564

Good Morning, Lord!

Good Morning, Lord!

George Shinn

HAWTHORN BOOKS, INC.
Publishers/NEW YORK

Library of Congress Catalog Card Number: 76-5716
ISBN: 0-8015-155769-72
 2 3 4 5 6 7 8 9 10

Foreword

If you are looking for an inspirational book, one that will lift you to higher levels of action and achievement, here it is: George Shinn's *Good Morning Lord*.

This book is written in a captivating narrative style that flows along, chapter by chapter, holding the reader's interest all the way. But it is more than an attractive writing style that holds one's fascinated attention throughout. The intense interest factor is the old, yet ever romantic, American story of a boy born in poverty who, through God's grace and his own faith and determination, overcomes one adversity after another to achieve outstanding success in life.

But even that dramatic factor is not the basic quality that grips the reader's sustained interest from the beginning to the end of this remarkable book. The fascinating element in this autobiography is the manner in which a young man, by complete commitment to Christ and with no apparent opportunity, forged the character and ability that now marks him as one of the notable younger contemporary laymen of the Christian community in this country.

The youngest man ever to receive the coveted and pres-
tigious Horatio Alger Award, given to those who have risen
from the humblest beginnings to positions of creative
achievement and service, George Shinn's story is a reminder
to all young persons now living in adverse circumstances
that they, too, can accomplish something very great in their
lives. This book shows how that can be done—at least how
one young man, who seemingly had nothing going for him,
did it.

But perhaps even this is not yet the profoundest element in
this inspired human story. That further element is this: The
author became highly successful in all his enterprises, but
from the beginning he dedicated himself to giving one-tenth
plus of his fortune to God's work. His relationship spiritually
has, from the start, been: "Lord, you direct and I will do the
work." It is, in effect, a close partnership, in which Mr.
Shinn prays for guidance in matters business and personal.
He takes no steps until he feels the Lord is directing the decision and will be in harmony with the Divine Will. Knowing
him intimately, I am aware of his complete and utter sincerity of purpose and attitude. Mr. Shinn regards himself as a
steward of God and honestly endeavors to administer his
wealth on that Christian basis. This book is an exciting illus-
tration of the dynamic truth that if a person gives himself
wholly to the Lord, the Lord is then able to work astonish-
ingly through that individual.

Personally, George Shinn is an engaging and delightful
man, full of life and fun. He possesses a sharp, keen mind
that, through a continuous prayer pattern, comes up with
remarkable insights. His grasp of situations, his innovative
procedures and acknowledged skills are impressive to all
who are in contact with him. Yet Shinn himself credits whatever know-how he possesses not to any outstanding ability
within himself but to the Lord. He believes that when one

truly commits himself to the Lord, the mind opens to God's leading, giving to the individual a mental power he would not otherwise possess.

I have, of course, known many dedicated people in my life and ministry but no one who is more genuinely sincere than this young business leader from North Carolina. His simplicity of faith, resulting in an exemplary life, his humble walk with God, his happy spirit, his insatiable desire to serve the Lord marks him as one of the rarest Christians of my experience. He is an eager, gifted, joyous disciple of the Lord Jesus Christ. If he remains always the same humble, unaffected, spiritually alive person, he will be one of God's most effective servants in our time.

If I seem to write with enthusiasm, it is because I have profound admiration for a man who commits himself so completely to Christ that one may discern with clarity the working of the Holy Spirit in his life and his work. I have sincere and affectionate regard for George Shinn, author of this strong motivational book, *Good Morning Lord*.

Norman Vincent Peale

Good Morning, Lord!

1

The auditorium was beautiful—the Starlight Roof of the Waldorf Astoria Hotel in New York. The date was Friday, October 17, 1975. I had stayed at the Waldorf previously on a couple of business trips, but mostly because the Waldorf was the only New York hotel I could think of when I got into a cab at the airport. Even then I was impressed by the place. I am a country boy, and a little elegance goes a long way with me.

But this time everything was different. I was on a stage with ten other American businesspeople, all of us recipients of the annual Horatio Alger Award. There was a time in my life when I would have been reluctant to call up these people on a business transaction. And now I was one of them. In front of us was an audience of almost a thousand, many of them earlier winners of the award, people whose names I had seen often in the leading business publications. They were giants, and they had taken the time to come here and witness the presentation. At the podium, ready to introduce the 1975 winners, was Dr. Norman Vincent Peale, a new friend and already a good friend. It was all so unreal, and I couldn't believe it.

A lot of people in the room that morning had one thing in common: We had once been poor and over the years we had worked our way up from rags to riches. That, to some degree, is what Horatio Alger Awards are all about. Sitting up there on the stage that morning, I was well aware that I had been poor, and for a long time. In fact, not being poor any more was so new to me that I still wasn't used to it.

The thought struck me that getting rich isn't all that difficult. Over the years, I had watched several businessmen become self-made millionaires, but they usually did it with such shotgun tactics that they would have landed in jail if they didn't have such clever lawyers. It didn't happen that way with me. Most of the time I couldn't afford a lawyer. Knowing that I would be expected to say a few words when I was given the award, I made up my mind that I was going to tell the audience the way it was with me. And the way it is. I looked around at the other recipients—one woman, nine men—and I wondered if their experience had been anything like mine. I soon found out.

Actually, I came close to not attending the presentation. Months earlier, I had received a letter from Helen Gray, the Executive Director of the Horatio Alger Awards Committee, informing me that I was being considered for an award and, unless I objected, representatives from the committee would investigate my past life. I didn't object; I just thought it wasn't going to be a very interesting assignment for the investigators. Also, I was sure there was no chance in the world for me to get the award. I couldn't figure out how I was even being considered. The likelihood of my winning seemed so remote that I put the subject out of my mind and didn't mention it to anyone for several days.

Then one morning I was having a sales conference with our key executives, some of whom had been with me since the beginning, and I realized that there were the people who would probably be interviewed if the investigation ever took place. So I told them about the letter and about the investigation, and I said: "If any of you is approached by these people, I just don't want you to say anything bad about me."

One man said: "George, if these people are going to check out your past life, there is no way that you will ever get that award—no way at all."

In our company, there is no room for ego trips, not even by the boss.

Time passed. One night some Raleigh neighbors came by and said they had been interviewed about life in the Shinn household. I asked them what they reported, and one woman said: "I just told them that your wife keeps beating you up."

Next, men at two or three companies we were doing business with called me to let me know they had been interviewed too, and one man said: "All I told them was that your credit rating was so bad, you've even been turned down by the Book-of-the-Month Club."

Then I got a call from my mother, who still lives in Kannapolis, where I was born and raised, and she said: "Junior, I hear there are some people going around town asking a lot of questions about you. What have you done now?"

"Nothing," I said. "It's all right, Mother. Some people in New York are just trying to find out if I should get a medal."

"What for?"

"I don't know."

"Well," she said, "it all sounds very strange."

I said: "It is."

Then there was nothing until September, when I got a phone call from Helen Gray. I suppose I got too excited because I misunderstood her. Anyway, I got the impression that candidates for the award had been narrowed down to eleven people and that I was one of them. Pleased, I went down the hall to the office of C. L. Jenkins, who is the administrator of a foundation I had recently set up, and I told him the good news.

Jenk said: "George, if you are one of the eleven finalists, then you are one of the winners."

I said: "No, Jenk. They don't give eleven awards."

"They sure do," he said. "After you told us about the award sometime back, I got a book about Horatio Alger and I read all about this. They've even given more than eleven. You're one of the winners, George."

"I don't believe it," I said. "But what do we do now?"

"Let's make sure," Jenk said. "I'll call Helen Gray." I stood there as he put through the call and explained the unclear situation. Then he asked: "Is George Shinn one of eleven finalists or one of eleven winners? He's a winner? Fine. Good. Thank you. What happens next? All right. What's the date of that? Good. We'll be there. Let us know if there is anything else we can do. Thank you. Goodbye." Jenk hung up and grinned at me and said: "Congratulations, Horatio Alger."

I was thrilled. I said: "I've never won anything before in my life. I want to tell Nick." Nick Galifianakis was a good friend who was also my personal lawyer. Earlier, he had served three terms in the United States Congress in the House, something he never let me forget. Now I had a chance for some bragging of my own. Nick was delighted by the news, but it seemed to me he wasn't overly impressed. Next, I thought of calling my wife, but then I decided it would be more fun to see her face when I told her what a distinguished husband she had.

Later in the day, Nick called me back and said: "George,

I've done some checking around. This Horatio Alger Award is a big deal."

"I don't know how big it is," I said. "I'm just glad that I got it."

"Well, it's big. There is only one other person from North Carolina who ever got it. Former Governor Luther Hodges."

All I could say to that was: "Wow."

"There's something else," he said, "but we'll have to check it out further. It looks like, at thirty-four, you are the youngest person ever to get the award. Most of the winners have been much older."

"I'll be doggone."

Nick said: "George, you people don't have a PR outfit working for you, do you?"

"No, we don't."

"I think you should get one. There is going to be a lot of mileage in this, both for the company and for yourself."

"Okay. We'll look into that."

"Another thing. I think you ought to get the presentation on film."

"Make a movie of it?"

"Why not? Twenty years from now you can show it to your kids."

"All right. I'll look into that, too. How about going up to New York with me for the big event?"

"You couldn't keep me away."

That evening when I got home I was very excited. My little boy ran up to me and I grabbed him and hugged him. I came up to my wife and picked her up and swung her around. That was quite a tussle because she was very much pregnant at the time. Then I told her with a great deal of enthusiasm: "Honey, I just won the Horatio Alger Award." She did not show any enthusiastic response. "Can you believe that I am the second person in North Carolina ever to get the award, next to a former governor of the state?" Still no enthusiasm. "Honey, do you realize that they searched the files and found out that I am the youngest ever to receive this distinguished award?"

My wife stepped back, looked at me, and said: "They should search the files a little bit more. You are probably also the shortest."

Pushing five-seven, if that, I have been razzed all my life about my height—or lack of it.

The public relations firm did a good job. Accounts of the award appeared on the television and radio news and in a lot of North Carolina newspapers. I might have felt like a celebrity, but nobody I knew would let me.

Helen Gray got in touch with us to find out how many rooms at the hotel we would want. I hadn't thought of that. I didn't think that the presentation would be any big affair, so I had planned to use the company plane to fly to New York that Friday morning, get the award, have lunch, then fly back to Raleigh. I realized, however, that this might be too much for Carolyn in her condition, so I decided to go up on Thursday and come back on Friday. We reserved five rooms—for Nick and his wife, Jenk, Carolyn and me, and the movie crew. I didn't see any reason for taking anybody else along, and still not used to having money, I didn't reserve anything swanky. This turned out to be a mistake, but perhaps a mistake understandable in a country boy.

After we checked into the Waldorf on Thursday, we were told that other winners, current and past, were holding receptions, and we were invited to wander around and meet people. To my chagrin, all the winners had taken elegant suites and brought along dozens of guests. One winner had a reception room as big as a ballpark, filled with famous people including Joe DiMaggio—one of my heroes. I felt like a hick and a cheapskate. Worse, I realized how much my mother and Carolyn's parents would have enjoyed all this and what a laugh my staff would have gotten out of seeing little George hobnobbing with all the big shots. But it was too late to do anything, so we just drifted about in a daze of hero worship.

On Friday, I awoke early, as I usually do, and I did what I have been doing the first thing in the morning for four years. I went to the window and looked out at the world and said aloud: "Good morning, Lord!" The first morning I had done that proved to be the turning point in my life.

Dr. Peale was to give out the awards alphabetically, which put me next to last; but I didn't want to hold up the works with the movie equipment, so I asked to be last. This gave me the chance to listen to the speeches of the other winners, and I found out that I was in my favorite kind of company.

—Helen F. Boehm, of Trenton, N.J., chairman of Edward Marshall Boehm, Inc., said that her formula for success was based on self, service and sincerity, and then she added: "But I found very early in life that there was another ingredient most important in my formula, and that was God. Of course, I never, never forgot Him in my recipe every day of my life."

—Edward E. Carlson, of Chicago, chairman of United Airlines, said: "I have a great feeling for the importance of a force greater than all of us, and that is the Lord and all of His preachings."

—R. J. Foresman, of Detroit, president of the Michigan General Corporation, said: "It takes a great many things combined for a better-than-average accomplishment. First of all, I think the good Lord has to have His hand on your shoulder. That's number one."

—Vincent G. Marotta, of Bedford Heights, Ohio, president of North American Systems, mentioned a Latin saying which he said his mother often quoted to him, and he explained: "It means have faith and hope in our Lord and you shall not be confounded."

—Robert L. Rice, of Salt Lake City, chairman of Health Industries, Inc., said: "I never let a day go by that I don't thank the good Lord for the opportunities that I've had."

—William G. Salatich, of Boston, president of Gillette North America, said: "I've been a very lucky man, lucky to be blessed by the Lord with so many things in so many ways."

And then it was my turn.

To begin with, I was born and raised in what was then the outskirts of Kannapolis, North Carolina. My father ran a gas station that was just across the road from our house, but it was more than that. My father sold groceries, and at certain times of the year the fresh vegetables he carried had been grown on our own property. The place had a pool table. Young men would hang around all evening, playing pool and sipping the cold soft drinks that were for sale. I am told that before I came along my father tried his hand at providing hard drinks but he got caught and almost landed in serious trouble.

I remember my father as being a gentle and loving man, hard-working and ambitious. My mother once told me: "Your father had only one weakness. He played poker. But when he lost, he was the only one who got hurt. He never once tried to cut into the money he gave me every week to run the house." Looking back, we were, I suppose, in comfortable means. We had a maid. Both my parents had been married once before. My father's first wife died; my mother's marriage ended in divorce. They both had children in the first marriages; but they all were much older than I was, mostly married and living elsewhere and I seldom saw them.

When I was around eight, my father decided to subdivide his property, build several one-family homes, and then sell the lots. He had to borrow a lot of money to get the project going, mortgaging everything he owned. First he had a street put in and he called it Irene Avenue, after my mother. And that was as far as he got. Before any more work could be done, he had a heart attack and died. He was fifty years old.

Even at eight, I understood what had happened, and I was stunned by the loss and the loneliness. For days, my mother and I couldn't look at each other without bursting into tears. On the day of the funeral, our minister came to the house afterwards, and he told me: "George, you will have to take care of your mother from now on."

"I know," I said, the tears streaming down my face. "I will. I promise you." Years had to pass before I could really make good on that promise.

We knew we had to go on. Not until the bills began coming in did we realize how rough going on was going to be. My father had died thousands of dollars in debt. To provide us with a living, my mother took over the gas station, even pumping the gas; but she had no experience in running a business, so she made some understandable mistakes, and in came more bills.

The creditors began going to court. Finally my mother was advised that she would have to consider filing for bankruptcy and that everything my father left would have to be auctioned off to pay the bills. I'll never forget the crushing humiliation of those auctions, watching other people make bids on what had been my father's life's work. The car went. The gas station went. The property went. Then the house was put on the block.

My mother wanted desperately to keep our home. She couldn't bid on it, of course, so she went to a friend and asked him to buy the house, promising that after he made the mortgage arrangements with the bank she would make the monthly payments. The man agreed, and then he went around telling people about the plan so that they would not bid against him. At the auction, my mother's surrogate at first appeared to be the only bidder; and if he could have gotten the house at the price he offered, it would have been a bargain. But there was a stranger in the crowd who started bidding. Up and up went the price. Then somebody took the stranger aside and explained to him what was going on, and he stopped bidding. So we at least had our home.

My mother had to go to work. For a while, she worked at the check-out counter of a supermarket. She also worked as a telephone operator at a time in our town when you still had to tell the operator what number you wanted. And she ran a motel. Because of my age and my size, there wasn't much I could do to help out. Later on, though, I got a job at a gas station washing cars. The customers paid a dollar and I got a piece of it. Obviously, I wasn't making much, but at least I didn't have to ask my mother for money whenever I wanted to go to the movies with my friends.

We were poor. And yet I don't remember ever giving much thought to that. I knew I had less than other kids had, but it never bothered me. As long as I had food to eat and clean clothes, I thought I was doing fine. Meals at our house were mostly beans and potatoes. If we were flush, on Sundays we had hamburgers or a meat loaf. I remember coming home one day after spending the afternoon at a friend's house, leaving there just as his mother began to prepare dinner. I told my mother: "Guess what the Millers are having for dinner. Steaks. Real steaks."

Mother looked me right in the eye and she said: "Well, that's all right, son. Steaks are beef; the hamburgers and meat loaf we sometimes have on Sunday are beef, too. Maybe the Millers just can't afford to have their beef ground up."

I bought that: I knew my mother would never deceive me. Actually, I didn't get around to eating a real steak until I was sixteen, at a season banquet for the high school football team I was on. I found that I preferred my mother's meat loaf.

The only incident which made our poverty cause me real embarrassment occurred when I was in fifth grade. The school I attended was two miles away, and I made the round trip everyday on the school bus. There wasn't time for most of the kids to go home for lunch, so we ate in the school cafeteria. My favorite girlfriend at the time was the prettiest and smartest girl in the class. She was a hall monitor, an honor student, and she also collected the lunch money everyday. You could pay by the day or by the week. I wasn't paying at all. My mother had gone to the county welfare office and explained our financial situation and it was arranged for me to get lunch free. One day the teacher asked how many kids had paid for lunch. The girl called out the number, then added: "And there are the two free lunches that go to George Shinn and Francis Craig."

I wanted to crawl under the woodwork. It didn't bother me that the teacher knew and the girl knew that I was getting lunch free, but I didn't expect my best girl to tell the whole world about it. I thought she knew better. At lunchtime, I didn't go to the cafeteria. Instead, I stalked out of the building and walked all the way home, furious, and I didn't go back to school in the afternoon. When my mother came home from work that evening and asked me how my day had gone, I told her what happened and I thought she would get as angry about it as I was.

But she got angry with me. She said: "Junior, you shouldn't have done that. Being poor is nothing to be ashamed of. But I'll be ashamed of you if you don't make something out of yourself so you can stop being poor."

That was small comfort at the moment. And that was the end of my fifth-grade romance.

Even then, I was sure I was going to make something out of my life, but I didn't know what. Because of my size, I learned early that the best way for me to avoid being trampled by the crowd was to get ahead of the crowd. I often did this by thinking fast and talking even faster and trying to make a joke out of everything. No matter what the situation was, I usually found myself running the show. Maybe it was because of my size that people let me get away with this. Maybe they figured it would be easy to hold me down in case I got too far out of line. Whatever, one result of the early experience was that I developed a great deal of self-confidence in my ideas and decisions. As a boy, I sometimes had to express my self-confidence with my fists. I never hesitated to do so, even if I had to get up on a ladder to do it. I didn't care if I lost; I just wanted to show that I wasn't afraid to fight.

Over the years, I have observed that many people are on treadmills not just because they are afraid to fight but mostly because they are afraid of losing. They are never sure that what they are about to say or do is the right thing, so they say and do nothing. As the Lord would have it, my life led me into a career of running business schools, and I have often been appalled by the lack of confidence some of the students have displayed. After at least two years of training by professionals, they still don't feel that they are ready to go out into the world and compete.

One such student was a girl named Clara. Clara was average, not brilliant; she was neat, but not pretty; she was easy going, not outgoing. As the school did with all graduates, we lined up a job interview for Clara as she was finishing the course. The morning of her interview, Clara came into my office clearly upset and nervous.

"Mr. Shinn," she said, "I can't go out on this interview."

"Why not?"

"I'd never get this job. The man is the president of the company."

"So what?"

"You know how big bosses are. They want a movie star."

"What's the good in hiring a movie star if she can't type or take shorthand? And you can do both."

"I couldn't pass a typing test this morning. I'm too flustered."

"You've been passing typing tests here for two years, Clara; otherwise, you wouldn't be graduating."

"I can't do it, Mr. Shinn. I just can't."

I thought about it. Then: "All right, Clara. I'll send somebody else out on this interview. But I'm going to line up another interview for you tomorrow, and I want you to go to it. In the meantime, I want you to think about something. When this school sends a student out on a job interview, it's our way of saying that we're proud of you and we have confidence in your abilities. You don't think we'd send out somebody who would make us look like we're running a junkyard here, do you? We have confidence in you, Clara. We think you can do any secretarial job that comes along. Now all you've got to do is acquire some confidence in yourself." She left.

A few days earlier, I had received a call from the general manager of a major company in town, asking me to find him a man who could be trained to become his office manager. I put in a call to him, and when he came on the line he said: "Hi, George. Have you found me a man yet?"

I said: "I'm going to send over a very capable person that I want you to interview."

"Who is he?"

"It's a she."

"George, I don't want a woman for this job. I want a man who can move into second place sooner or later."

"I know that, Jim," I said, "but I want you to meet this girl as a favor to me. She's very capable, but she doesn't believe that yet. She has no confidence in herself. I think it would be good for her to have a couple of interviews just for the experience."

"Like a dry run?"

"Yes, sort of. I'd appreciate it if you'd see her."

"All right. Send her over."

Next morning when Clara came into my office, I handed her a piece of paper with the man's name and address, and this time she was not nervous. She was smiling, confident and overflowing with enthusiasm.

Leaving, she stopped at the door and said: "I will get that job today; I have confidence. Mr. Shinn, I'm going to make you proud of me."

I didn't have the heart to tell her this was just a dry run. I said: "Better still, Clara, make you proud of yourself." She left. For over an hour, I sweated, hoping that Clara would get something beneficial from the interview.

Then the man called me, and he asked: "Are you sure you sent me the right girl?"

"Was her name Clara?"

"That's what she said."

"Then it was the right girl."

"Well," he said, "she didn't come off the way you described. I was expecting a timid hummingbird; the girl who walked into this office was full of confidence and enthusiasm. She almost broke a couple of my fingers when we shook hands."

"Really?"

"I'm telling you. We talked for a few minutes, and then I asked her: 'Clara, are you a fast typist?' And she said with confidence: 'Yes, sir, I can do seventy words a minute—without a mistake.' So I said: 'This job requires someone who is good at shorthand.' And she said: 'I can do a hundred and twenty words a minute—without a mistake.' Then I told her: 'Well, for this important position we need somebody who is excellent at accounting.' And Clara leaned up to my desk and said: 'I can open and close a complete set of books—without a mistake.' I couldn't believe that someone with no experience could be so confident. So I asked her one more question, and then I hired her."

I asked: "What was the question?"

He said: "I asked her: 'Clara, do you lie?' She smiled, looked me right in the eyes and said: 'No, sir, but I can learn.' "

Clara had done herself proud.

Self-confidence can help you overcome all kinds of obstacles, and I know an excellent case in point. Here in North Carolina, Benny was a young black who was transferred to an all-white high school in the early days of forced integration. Benny loved football and had his heart set on making the school's team. He had three things going against him. First, he was black. Second, he was not a large person—around five-seven and maybe a hundred sixty pounds. Third, he was surrounded by negativism: his relatives and friends kept telling him that he didn't have a chance because of his race.

Even so, Benny was there for the tryouts, and he took a lot of punishment from the other boys as they all went through the coach's drills. He didn't make it. Undaunted, he went up to the coach and asked if he could be the team's waterboy, and the coach said yes. Benny was there for every practice session, watching everything. After the team left, Benny stayed at the field until dark, running, doing calisthenics, beating himself to a pulp at the tackling dummies. Everytime the coach gave a talk in the locker room analyzing plays, Benny was there, taking notes and memorizing every play. Throughout the season, Benny never missed a session. He thought about football all the time, yet kept his grades up so that he wouldn't have any problem about them later on.

The next year when the tryouts were called, Benny was there. His self-confidence and his hard work made him look like a superstar compared to the other boys. He made the team. Furthermore, he was selected the most valuable player by his teammates. He went on to make the all-county team, the all-conference team and finally all-state his senior year. On top of that, he won a college football scholarship.

Self-confidence is simply having faith in your abilities, your talents. How do you find out what your talents are? I think that many people are aware of their talents, their proclivities, early in life. Doctors have told me that when they were kids they were already dissecting field mice. A couple of writers have told me that they were at it in grammar school just for fun, not realizing that they were setting the pattern of their lives. Business friends have shared with me memories of how inventive they were as kids in creating part-time jobs for themselves. It shows early. But no matter how old you are, once you determine where you want to go, your future depends on what you are willing to do to sharpen your talents so that they become mature, competitive and professional. It may mean school, as it did with Clara. It may mean a lot of practice, as it did with Benny. It will certainly mean a lot of hard work, discipline and dedication before the time comes when you can have the confidence of knowing that you know your job.

And there is something else. In order to develop faith in your talents, you must also develop faith in the source of all talents—the Lord. Philippians 4:13 tells us: "I can do all things through Christ which strengtheneth me." This immediately changes the ground rules: you achieve not only on your abilities but also on your conscience. You have got to function within the Lord's laws or you will not keep whatever you may gain.

It took me a long time to learn this, but I did have an experience as a boy that sent me off in the right direction. My buddies and I discovered one summer that the best watermelons growing in the area were on a farm about a mile from where we lived. We started going there about twice a week, helping ourselves to the best melons, and going into the woods for a feast. One Saturday afternoon, as we were finishing up a ball game, I told the boys to meet me at this place in the woods on Sunday night just as it was growing dark for another party.

The next morning, I went to church as usual with my mother. The preacher went into a long and angry tirade about the evils of stealing, not only stealing things that didn't belong to you but stealing a man's reputation by trying to damage it or even stealing from our own lives by wasting time. He had many other examples, any one of which, he said, would bring down the wrath of God upon us. He went on and on. I began to squirm. I sat there knowing perfectly well that I had a date that night to steal some more watermelons.

Ordinarily, when we got home, I would have changed my clothes and gone out to look for my friends. This Sunday, I changed my clothes, but I stayed home, loafing around the house all day, suffering, ready at any moment to have the wrath of God hit me like a ton of bricks. My mother asked me several times if something was wrong. I told her no, that I just didn't feel like going out. And I didn't.

It began to get dark. I knew that my friends would be gathering in the woods, waiting for me, but I couldn't bring myself to leave the house. Finally it occurred to me that I at least had to go out there, and I promised myself that I wouldn't steal any melons, that I wouldn't eat any that they did, and that I would never suggest to my friends that we steal any more.

I went out there. The place was pitch dark. I didn't see any of my friends, so I figured that they had already been there, stolen the melons, had a feast, then gone off somewhere else. I was about to leave when I heard a noise in the bushes. I went and looked. There was one of my friends, squatting down.

Annoyed, I asked: "What are you doing here?"

He said: "Don't ask." And he groaned.

I heard other groans and began to move about. I found the other boys, five or six of them, all squatting and all sick. I asked one boy: "What's going on?"

He said: "The farmer came out here and caught us just finishing the melons."

"Was he mad?"

"No. He laughed his head off."

"What for?"

"He said he had a feeling today that we were coming back tonight, so this afternoon he went to his watermelon patch and loaded up all the best melons with croton oil."

"Oh, no."

"Oh, yes. I'm living proof."

I said: "Come on, let's get out of here."

He said: "Not yet. I'm afraid to move. I think my whole insides are coming out."

I left by myself, grateful that my conscience had saved me from a fate worse than death.

My best friend when I was growing up was Glenn Compton. Actually, Glenn did more growing up than I did. He shot up to six feet tall by the time we were in junior high school and he took on a few more inches after that. His weight leveled off at around 300, all of it strength. I stood just to about Glenn's shoulders; he could have picked me up with one hand, and occasionally he did. Although we were the best of friends, Glenn and I had our arguments, and we would go through brief periods of avoiding each other. This was not easy to do. We lived near each other in a rural area; Glenn's father, like mine, had died young; Glenn's mother and my mother were good friends, so sooner or later we would run into each other, acknowledge each other with a nod, and then pick up where we had left off as though nothing had happened.

There were two things I would never argue about with Glenn—girls and sports. With girls, there really wasn't much to compete about. Girls who liked Glenn's type wouldn't give me a second glance. Girls were usually attracted to me because I was little and they could mother me. But if Glenn took a fancy to one of my girls, I never tried to deter him. That would have been suicide.

Sports were something else. With sports, I always tried to see to it that Glenn and I were on the same side. For me to try to ward off this giant at basketball would have been even more suicidal than trying to take a girl away from him. Tackling him at football or being tackled by him would have meant broken bones for me, for sure. Even at baseball, Glenn could almost play the outfield all by himself; and when he hit one to the outfield, it came at you like a bullet. So, whatever sport, Glenn and I were on the same side or I wouldn't play.

We kids loved athletics. I went fishing only once as a kid; and after hours of not catching anything, I decided not to waste any more time at that sport. However, I did go fishing once more, as a man, on vacation at Myrtle Beach, South Carolina, surf-fishing. I'm sure I caught the smallest fish in the Atlantic Ocean. I threw it back.

My friends and I spent all of our free time at sports. Rarely did we ever have enough kids get together for real teams— nine at baseball, eleven at football, whatever—but that didn't stop us. We thought that touch football was for girls; even though we didn't have any uniforms, we played football for real, broken bones or no broken bones. That's why I had to have Glenn Compton on my team.

I was never very much of a student. After spending all day in school, I didn't see the sense in taking home a lot of books and spending all evening at schoolwork. I took home books only to please my mother, but I never looked at them. I was too restless, I had a great need for activity, I couldn't fall asleep at night unless I had the feeling that I had been the winner at something during the day.

This changed slightly when I got into high school. In North Carolina, the biggest sport in high school is football. Make the football team and you are automatically something of a hero. I wanted very much to be a hero, especially as far as the girls were concerned. But then I discovered that I really knew next to nothing about football.

One day, as the tryouts for the school team were coming up, I was with Glenn and a friend of ours from grammar school named Danny Little. We were talking about what positions we were going to try out for, and Glenn said: "I'm going out for tackle." I figured that with his build he could have any position he wanted. He asked me: "What are you going out for?"

The only position I knew by name was quarterback, so I said: "I'm going out for quarterback."

Danny Little was two years older than I was and in much stronger physical shape. He said: "I'm going out for quarterback. Why don't you go out for end?"

I asked: "What's end?" My cow-pasture football was showing its shortcomings.

Danny said: "When a play is called, the end works his way around the other team and gets into the clear. Then the quarterback throws him a forward pass and he runs down the field and makes a touchdown."

That sounded heroic enough. I said: "Okay, I'll go out for end."

I didn't know that a good end needed some height; so when I showed up at the tryouts for end, I saw that not only were more boys trying out for this position than any other but that I was the smallest of them all. But I had something going for me. When you are small, it helps to be fast, and I was fast. It was my speed, then, that landed me on the team as a first-string end. The following year when I again went out for end, the coach said: "Shinn, because you can move as fast as you do, I'm putting you in at halfback. You can play end when the regular end can't play for some reason."

I was soon to learn that a good halfback was two or three times my size, but it didn't matter. As long as I could be on the team with Glenn and Danny, as long as I could be out there in the thick of the fight, I was happy, no matter how many times I found myself at the bottom of a heap of bodies scrambling for the ball. I loved it.

When you are young and full of ambitions and day-dreams, you are undergoing experiences that are shaping you as an adult, and, sadly, you are usually an adult before you recognize this and utilize it, if you do at all. As a boy, I learned to be self-motivated, to be a self-starter. I don't think my size had anything to do with it. I didn't give any more thought to the fact that I was short than I did to the fact that I was poor. These are circumstances that I acknowledged and then forgot about. I just knew that it was urgent for me to achieve. It took me a long time to realize that self-motivation was simply a daydream with muscles on it.

I also came to realize that there is no such thing as a "born" self-starter. Experiencing motivation is a conscious act, a matter of thought, decision and action in the process of reaching a specific goal. Having goals, then, is the first step in developing motivation. The person who has no goals, who is satisfied with what he's got and where he is going, is bound to get into a rut and stay there, achieving nothing. Nelson Rockefeller should certainly have been satisfied with what he had, but he had a goal of becoming President of the United States. He hasn't made it yet, but he has come as close to it as he can get, and in the process of doing so he has spent most of his adult life in important public service, achieving a lot for himself and his country.

A few years ago, I remember, one of the graduates of our

business college in Raleigh got a job in the secretarial pool of a large company, starting at $100 a week. She soon learned that some of the girls around her were making as much as $175. She called me about it, saying: "I think it's unfair for the company to expect me to start for such a low salary when I'm doing just as much work as the other girls and I'm doing it just as well."

I pointed out: "Betty, the other girls have been working there longer than you and have probably been getting regular raises right along. You'll get yours in time, I'm sure. Of course, if you want to see the raises coming along sooner, you can't just do as well as the other girls—you'll have to do better."

"In what way?" she asked.

I asked: "What time do you get to work in the morning?"

"Nine o'clock."

"How long does it take you to settle down and get going?"

"Maybe ten or fifteen minutes."

"Then why don't you get to work ten or fifteen minutes earlier so that you can be turning out your work at nine? That's what you're getting paid for. Do you get coffee breaks?"

"Two. Fifteen minutes in the middle of the morning, and fifteen minutes in the middle of the afternoon."

"Is it essential to your mental and physical health that you go out for coffee everytime?"

"I don't go for coffee; I don't like coffee. I have a Coke."

"Would it be possible to sip your Coke at your desk while you continue to work?"

"I suppose so."

"That way you could be adding another half hour a day to your production. How much time do you have for lunch?"

"An hour."

"How long does it take to go out for lunch?"

"Around forty minutes."

"And then what do you do?"

"Usually I read a newspaper."

"Well, I'm all for people keeping up with the latest news. Can you read a whole newspaper in that amount of time?"

"I don't try. I just read enough to kill the time."

"You wouldn't have to kill time if you went back to work earlier. What time do you quit for the day?"

"Five."

"I mean, what time do you head for the powder room to get ready to leave?"

"Oh. About a quarter to five, sometimes a little earlier. It gets crowded in there."

"Why don't you wait until after five? It wouldn't be so crowded. What I'm getting at, Betty, is that if you let your boss see that you like your job, that you enjoy the work and that you are willing to make an extra effort to increase your production, I'm sure the raises will start coming in before long."

She thought about it. Then: "What happens if I do what you say and I don't get any raise?"

"Then quit. Your boss has responsibilities to you just as you have responsibilities to him. If you are working for people who don't see and appreciate your extra effort, you are working for the wrong people."

"I'll think about it," she said.

I didn't hear from Betty again for four months, until one Sunday morning when I saw her at her church where I had gone to give a talk. Joking, I asked: "Are you making one-seventy-five yet?"

"Not yet," she said, "but I'm getting close. One-fifty."

I said: "That's a wonderful raise in such a short time. How did it happen?"

"Well," she said, "I did what you suggested—made the extra effort, but nothing happened for several weeks. Then one of the personal secretaries in the office got married, and she took her two-week vacation time to go on her honeymoon. I asked the supervisor of the secretarial pool if I could fill in for the girl, and I was told yes but only if I could keep up with most of my own work at the same time. It was a real grind but I did it."

"And that's how you got the raise?"

"Not exactly. The girl who got married decided to become a housewife, so she quit her job. Her boss had gotten to like me during those two weeks, so he asked me to become his personal secretary. That's how I got the raise."

"Good for you," I said. "See what a little motivation can do? I'll bet you'll be getting the one-seventy-five before you know it."

"Oh, I've got bigger plans now," she said, laughing. "I'm aiming for two hundred."

I don't know if she got it but presumably she did. If she ever had another reason to become unhappy with the company, I'm sure I would have heard about it.

Another good example of motivation is Bob Hodge, now an executive with our company in charge of student recruitment in high schools. Bob was thirty when he decided to become a student himself in our Raleigh school, King's College. Before then, Bob had worked for a printing company for a dozen years, eventually earning around ten thousand a year, but he knew that he had reached the end of the line on the job he had. His wife, Ruth, meanwhile, who was a graduate of King's, had an administrative job in business that paid her almost as much as Bob was earning, and her future was still wide open. Between them, they certainly had a pretty good family income for a young couple. But Bob was more concerned about his personal growth as an individual and a businessman, so he decided to seek a new career while he was still young enough to get ahead in whatever field it might be. A veteran, he quit his job and entered the college on the G.I. Bill.

Two years passed. One day I got a call from Britt Dorman, president of the college, and he said: "As you know, George, we're looking for someone to add to our staff of recruiters for the high school market. Well, we've got a student here now who I think is just the man."

"Wouldn't he be kind of young?"

"Not really." And Britt gave me Bob's background, letting me know that Bob would be graduating in a few weeks. Then he said: "We're having elections here for the student government, and there's going to be a big rally this afternoon. Bob is campaign manager for one of the candidates, so he will be one of the speakers. I think you should come over and hear his talk."

As Britt and I took places in the back of the building that afternoon, a girl was making an impassioned speech on behalf of her candidate. She got a pretty good hand. Then an older-looking student stepped to the microphone and began. Britt said: "That's Bob Hodge."

He had a good appearance, a pleasant voice. He was calm and confident. He was sincere, persuasive, and he was doing a very effective soft-sell on his candidate. I looked around. The audience was transfixed. A lot of the students were still in their teens; most of the others were ten or twelve years younger than Bob, and yet they all sat there listening to him intently, laughing at his occasional and well-timed jokes, as though he was one of them. And, in a way, he was, speaking to them as one of them, with respect for their intelligence, their maturity, their individuality.

Britt whispered: "What do you think?"

I said: "I like him. I think he can do the job. Get together with him."

The next day, Britt called and said that Bob was definitely interested, depending on salary. When the time came to talk money, I told Bob: "We can't start you off at the ten thousand you were getting at the printing company; but if you have the kind of motivation that this job needs, your salary will go up, and you can be sure there will be no limit to what you can earn."

He said: "Let's give it a try."

He gave it a sensational try. His genius for communicating with the young virtually turned him into the Pied Piper of Hamelin. Before long, most of the students coming to us directly from high schools came through Bob. He was so good that we sent him out to recruit for other schools that we owned and, eventually, other schools we were serving as consultants. The time came when we could set up a special department for high school recruiting, with Bob at the head of it, earning more than he ever had before, and with his future still wide open.

Not long ago, a North Carolina politician started coming around our office every once in a while on short visits. We all liked him and enjoyed his visits, but I kept waiting for him to ask me for a campaign contribution. Instead, one day he said: "George, let me tell you why I like coming here. It's the atmosphere. Everybody is so friendly, so outgoing, and filled with such good spirits. When I come down the hall, your men don't just look up from their desks and smile and nod hello. They get up and come to the door and we shake hands. I don't get treated like that anywhere else. What's so special around here?"

"There's a lot special around here," I said. "In the first place, people don't work here long before they learn that the best way to get anyplace is to get up off your rear and get moving. We get off our rears real fast around here. Second, everybody around here is always glad to see you and enjoys talking to you—you make us feel good, so that part is no act. Third, we are all so excited about the way the company is growing that we keep going at top speed so that we don't miss out on anything. Fourth, we know that the Lord is giving us many blessings; and we know that if we don't put out our best efforts all the time to fulfill His plans as fast as He shows them to us, we won't deserve them and would stop getting the blessings. Basically, it's the Lord who creates the atmosphere around here. Believe me, it was a far different place before He started doing so."

Isaiah 40:31 tells us: "They who wait for the Lord shall renew their strength, they shall mount up with wings like eagles, they shall run and not be weary, they shall walk and not faint."

Motivation, then, is a total of trust in your abilities; a desire to improve; distinct goals; the eagerness to put out the extra effort necessary to reach them; and receptiveness to God's guidance, which you develop by keeping the Lord in mind in everything that you do.

I must admit, however, that the Lord was not always included in my own motivations. In high school, for example, I knew perfectly well that the main reason I wanted to be on the football team was that girls liked football players. Another feature girls liked about the male peacock was thick hair styled into a ducktail. That I had. But I had a tough time trying to shine as a football star. As halfback, I spent most of my time disappearing under mounds of male bodies and I was seldom seen by the stands. And the coach would let me play only when the team was so far ahead or so far behind that anything I did wouldn't make much difference. I was playing one game when I was sure my moment had come.

The play had been called. I broke into the clear and raced

down the field, turning just in time to catch the pass. Before I could take a step, I was tackled in midair by the whole opposition team. I dropped to the ground. The ball slipped out of my grasp. And my helmet flew off. When I was finally able to get to my feet, the first thing I did was comb my hair with my hands. Then I retrieved my helmet, put it on and trotted back to the scrimmage line.

A few days later, the team was watching movies that had been made of the game. At one point, the coach turned off the projector and said: "Now, men, I want you to watch this next play carefully. It is the best demonstration I have ever seen of the kind of fighting spirit that makes a great football player and a great team."

He turned on the machine. It was the play where I had lost my helmet. The team watched in silence. The coach turned off the machine and said: "Men, I want you to watch that play again. Notice the player's deep concentration on the game, his amazing determination to win."

He turned on the machine, this time running it backwards and in slow motion. When it got to the part where I took the time to fix my hair, everybody in the room broke up except me. I sank low in my chair.

The coach turned the machine off and looked at me. He said: "Shinn, maybe you will get someplace in life despite everything. But it won't be in football."

Then he turned on the machine and I had to sit through the whole humiliation again.

I didn't graduate with my high school class. It was my own fault. For some reason, maybe because I inwardly suspected that I really didn't shine much either as a student or an athlete, I usually had to resort to pranks to get attention. Anything for a laugh. In my senior year, I wasn't on the football team anymore; but the players were all good friends of mine and I spent a lot of time with them. One day at school we had a pep rally in the assembly; all the players were in the first two rows. There were cheers and songs and pep talks, and everybody got excited.

After the rally, the students were told to go directly to their next class, which for me was English, a subject I always had trouble with. The players were told it would be all right for them to be late to class. Carried away, I suppose, I didn't go to class but went instead with some of the players to the student lounge and joked with them for a few minutes. One of the players was in my English class, and we took our time getting there. When we finally got there, we each put an arm around the other's shoulders and paraded into the room singing the school's fight song at top voice.

The kids laughed, but the teacher didn't think it was funny. She told the two of us to go to the principal's office. I was the one who was in real trouble: I should have gone directly to class. Besides, teachers had been sending me to the principal's office so much lately that the place was beginning to feel like my second home. The last time, the principal warned me that one more visit by me and I would be thrown out of school. I couldn't bring myself to face that threat, real or not. Instead of going to the principal's office, I went into the library.

As my luck would have it, the teacher came into the library and saw me. She came over to me and asked: "George, what did the principal say to you?"

It would have been useless to lie. I said: "I didn't go to the principal, ma'am."

She began to boil. "Why not?"

"I figured I was in enough trouble already."

"Well, there's going to be more," she said. "Come with me." And she led me to the principal's office.

I wasn't thrown out of school, but I was thrown out of the English class for the rest of the semester, which was just about the same. The expulsion meant that I wouldn't have enough credits to graduate with my class and that I would have to go to summer school to get my diploma. I didn't go to my class's commencement exercise. I felt lousy enough as it was.

I finally got my high school diploma, and I was ready to look for a full-time job. I had wanted to go to college; but there wasn't any money for it, I figured I would work for a couple of years, save my money, and then go to college. But then I did something that forced me to change my plans. I bought a used car. The thing was forever breaking down, and I was putting my money into it as fast as I earned it.

In Kannapolis, the biggest employer was—and still is—the Cannon Mills Company. There is no relationship between the name of the town and the name of the company, although many people think there is. It just so happened that, years back, a family named Cannon opened a mill in our town and became very successful. The mill usually needed help, so if a person really wanted to work he went over there. Glenn Compton was already working there. Glenn could have gotten an athletic scholarship to just about any college in the country he wanted; but even free tuition would nevertheless have continued to make him a financial burden on his family for living expenses, and he didn't want that. Glenn and I did the same kind of work at the mill—lugging around heavy bolts of fabrics which machines turned into different products. It was hard work but all it required was muscle power, so Glenn and I were still able to talk a lot about sports and cars and girls.

I wasn't working at the mill long when I became aware of something that puzzled me. A lot of people were unhappy with their jobs to the point of being miserable. It wasn't the company's fault. These same people were unhappy about everything in their lives. When I'd get fed up with the complaints, I'd ask these people why they didn't do something to change things. I got a variety of answers, but they all had a common thread. Like: "I don't know how to do any other kind of work." Or: "I'm too old to try to get a fresh start in something else." Or: "I can't afford to be out of work a week, so I don't have time to jobshop." Or: "My health isn't too good. What chance would I have?"

It seemed to me that all these people were just making excuses for their mental, physical and spiritual lassitude. They had no faith in themselves; and so they were filled with worries, doubts and fears. I swore that I would never let this happen to me, and I haven't. Nobody has to.

When I was in high school, I had a slight stammer that was most noticeable when I was called on in class and had to speak. At times, it was really embarrassing. After a while, I noticed that some of my teachers didn't call on me as much as they called on other kids. I had a good idea why the teachers were doing that, and I didn't like it. I wasn't a brilliant student by any means; but I wasn't an idiot either, and I didn't like sitting through class after class as though I was a visitor. Also, I faced the fact that probably the reason why I stammered was that I realized inwardly that I hadn't done my homework and didn't know the answers. Stammering, then, was like an impulsive crutch which allowed me to kill time while I tried to think of what to say. I didn't want to go through life like that. So I went to some of the teachers and told them that I wished they would call on me more often. A couple of teachers indicated the reason why they weren't calling on me—they felt sorry for me. That I didn't need.

I told them: "You shouldn't have told me that. Now I'll never study at all. But I'm sure that if I know there's a chance that I'll be called on from time to time, I'll make more of an effort to be prepared."

After that, it seemed to me that I was spending most of my class time on my feet, talking away. The stammer quickly disappeared. In fact, the day came when one teacher told me: "You'd be a better student, George, if you could only learn when to shut up."

The years have taught me that worries, doubts and fears can become insurmountable roadblocks in a person's personal growth and career advancement. Although these attitudes are products of the mind, usually without an actual basis, they can become very real, freezing you mentally, physically and spiritually. At the heart of the matter is an unrealistic and a negative appraisal of your own potential. I once read a piece of advice attributed to that famous philosopher Anonymous, and it went like this:

"He who knows and knows that he knows is a man. Follow him.

"He who knows and knows not that he knows is asleep. Wake him up.

"He who knows not and knows that he knows not is a student. Teach him.

"He who knows not and knows not that he knows not is a fool. Keep away from him."

Most of us, I think, are always something of a student. We become sleepers when we don't really know ourselves. But each one of us can become a real man. It all boils down to the ingredient that distinguishes the student from the sleeper: Faith.

When I was a small boy, I spent a part of every summer at Vacation Bible School. The purpose of the school was, of course, to bring the kids closer to the Lord, but I am sure that most of us attended just to meet new friends and have some fun. One day, the minister opened a study session by holding up a dollar bill and saying: "I will give this dollar to anybody who will come up here and accept it." The kids just looked at each other. Nobody moved. At that point in my life, I had never had a whole dollar to myself and, since nobody else moved, I decided I'd be crazy to pass up this opportunity to get rich. I got up. I walked to the minister and put out my hand. He gave me the dollar. I put it in my pocket and went back to my place and sat down.

The minister said: "Boys and girls, George Shinn has just

given us a demonstration in faith. I said I would give the dollar to anybody who would come up here and accept it. George believed in me, and now he has the dollar. Boys and girls, God is offering you a good life in this world and the next; and all you have to do to get it is show Him that you believe in Him by going to Him and asking Him for His blessings."

That didn't make much of an impression at the moment. All I cared about was that I had a dollar in my pocket and I couldn't wait to spend it. But, years later, a day came when I very much needed a dollar, and it wasn't until then that I recognized the wisdom in the minister's analogy.

Worry and doubt, I would say, are akin to fear, and, my dictionary says, fear is an "uneasy feeling that something may happen contrary to one's desires." As such, fear can have certain values. For instance, I want to live and I don't want to kill anybody else, so it is a kind of fear that makes me a careful driver. Also my father and my stepbrother both died young from heart attacks, evidence enough to make me fearful and worrisome, attitudes I was able to overcome when I made a habit of going to my doctor for regular medical check-ups. It seems to me, then, that a fear that stirs you to take some positive action is a good fear. But the fear that freezes you, that fills you with such doubts about yourself that you won't make a move of any kind, is the kind of fear that can literally destroy you. Fear is real. Fear is the second most powerful force in the world. The most powerful force is faith.

Psalms 34:4 tells us: "I sought the Lord, and He answered me, and delivered me from all my fears." It doesn't say a few of my fears; it says all of my fears. But it also doesn't say that all you've got to do is seek the Lord, dump all your problems on Him, and then forget about it all. That uneasy feeling that something may happen contrary to one's desires may well grow out of the fact that one's desires are not what the Lord would desire for you. The businessman who goes into a negotiations meeting with every intention of beating the other side to a pulp would either be a fool or a hypocrite if he expected the Lord to help him. If you want the Lord's help, you've got to do things the Lord's way.

Usually the best way to conquer a fear is to face it head on and challenge it. When I was a small boy, I remember, my mother had a habit of leaving a light on in the hall at night so that I could see my way in case I woke up and had to go to the bathroom. From time to time, the bulb would burn out and I would awaken in the darkness, suddenly so terrified that I would not go to the bathroom and often couldn't fall back to sleep until dawn. This fear bugged me for years. In junior high school, I found a new friend who started inviting me to spend the night at his house, but I kept thinking up excuses why I couldn't. I knew perfectly well why: I'd be expected to sleep in the dark and I felt I couldn't. I thought about it, and I faced the fact that I was getting a little old for this childishness, so I accepted the invitation. When the time came to go to bed, my friend led me to the room I was to use, he said good night and left, closing the door. For a moment, I thought of leaving the light on all night, but then I realized that this would seem very strange to any member of the family who might catch me at it. So when I was ready I turned off the light and got into bed. I didn't get much sleep that night, but with each passing hour in the darkness my fear grew less and less until it was gone. I almost felt it leave my body, and I was greatly relieved. And I was proud of myself for not resorting to the flashlight I had brought along with me in my overnight bag—just in case.

Sometimes people need a crisis to let the rest of us see them as they really are, often getting the first real look themselves, and I remember a vivid example. Working across the road at the gas station that used to be my father's was a man around thirty who had a short and slight build. He was easygoing, he never had much to say for himself, and he always seemed ready to go to any lengths to avoid a confrontation even of the mildest kind. The neighborhood feeling was that he was very timid, and we called him the Little Coward behind his back.

One summer evening just at sunset, I was home, and I heard an ear-splitting crash on the highway. I hurried outside. There had been a car collision, and one car had rolled onto its side. Flames were already appearing on the underside. Other people came out of their homes. Cars stopped and passengers got out. We could all hear the trapped driver screaming for help. But we all stood there, helpless, afraid, knowing that the car could explode any moment.

Suddenly out of the gas station at top speed came the Little Coward, running to the burning car without hesitation. He tried to open the door on the upturned side but couldn't. He climbed up onto the car and pulled at the door but it was jammed. He broke the window by stomping on the glass with his heavy boots, the flames rising around him. Then he hoisted from the car a man twice his size. The rest of us could see that the driver had lost an arm in the collision. The Little Coward carried the man to safety and placed him gently on the ground just as the ambulance he'd already had the foresight to call arrived and just as the car exploded.

The ambulance attendant told the Little Coward to get into the ambulance, too, but he kept insisting that he was all right. The attendant said: "Look at those burns you've got. You're practically cooked. Get in." He got in. We learned later that his burns were severe but the burns did not stop him from proving what a person can do with a tremendous amount of faith.

After that, we didn't call him the Little Coward anymore. We called him the Silent Giant, and we called him that to his face. He had done something none of the rest of us on the scene had the faith in our potentials to dare: he had risked his life in order to save somebody else's life. The Bible tells us that the greatest love is to be ready to lay down your life for your friend. The Silent Giant had done it for a complete stranger.

Fortunately, few of us are called upon to test our inner strengths in such life-threatening circumstances. Maybe more of us would be ready to risk it if we had a better idea what our inner strengths were. We never know what we can do until we try. If we fail, if we make a mistake, so what? That's why they put erasers on pencils. At least we can find out something about ourselves, and that's one subject none of us can know too much about. But we aren't going to learn much if we don't have the right attitude—the positive, aggressive, creative attitude. If you think on the bright side, you will live on the right side. If you think in the shadows, you will live in the shadows.

I remember, while I was still in high school, about fifteen of us guys chipped in to rent a cottage at the beach for a week. None of us could cook, so we ate out or brought back sandwiches. Late one night, we were all hungry but we couldn't find a place open where we could buy food. We decided to make a search of the cottage, just in case some previous tenant had left behind anything edible. In a lower drawer in the pantry off the kitchen, two of the boys found a box of Saltine crackers. Knowing that there wasn't enough for all of us, each boy ate several crackers in the darkened pantry, then put the crackers back, not saying anything. I noticed, though, that they weren't so intent on finding food as they had been. Then another boy found the box and brought it out into the light. We saw the few remaining crackers in the box. We also saw that the box was loaded with ants. We showed the box to the two gluttons so they could see what they had eaten. Their reactions were totally opposite, with a significance I never forgot. One boy turned green and rushed outside and upchucked for an hour, suffering without giving a thought to the probability that he had eaten something harmless. The other boy laughed and said: "Well, great. I didn't know that I was having such a well-balanced meal—meat with my crackers."

Along the same idea that people often get exactly what they're looking for is the experience of a friend of mine who told me recently that he had been happily married for seventeen years—except in one area. From the beginning, his wife had been waking him up in the middle of the night two or three times a week, saying that she had heard noises downstairs and telling him to go down and see if there was a burglar in the house. At first he thought she was serious, so, without grumbling, he got up each time and went to look. He never came upon a burglar, he never saw any signs of entry, and nothing was ever missing. But as this went on, year after year, my friend got fed up with it, and there were frequent middle-of-the-night spats until the woman started crying and threatening to go home to mother and my friend, grumbling a lot, got up and went to look. Nothing.

Recently it happened again. Again there were the spat, the tears and the threats, and my grumbling friend got up and went downstairs. He saw nothing, until he opened the door to the den and clicked on the light. There was a burglar, revolver in hand. My friend said: "Now, mister, listen. Let's not have any trouble. Help yourself to whatever you want, and I promise you I won't call the police. But before you go, I want you to do me a favor. Come upstairs, I want you to meet my wife. She's been waiting for you for seventeen years."

Like my friend, we all have problems, and we have problems in every area of life. There is no way to escape this. Furthermore, the bigger you become in your career, the bigger your problems are going to be. How you solve your problems and how you learn to live with problems that can't be solved are parts of the growing process and add up to you, to what you are as an individual. Letting yourself become addicted to worries and doubts and fears is like inviting cancer to take over your life.

Several years ago, I went through a period when I seemed to be picking up a new problem every hour of the day. As the problems accumulated, I reached a point where I was virtually worrying myself sick. I knew I needed advice, and so I went to Dr. Gilmore W. Johnson for it. He was an honors graduate from Wake Forest University, a Phi Beta Kappa, a man with over twenty-five years of experience in education, an Educational Distinguished Service Award recipient, and honorary doctorate recipient, and a true Southern gentleman. I had great respect and admiration for him, and I felt that he, if anyone, could help me. I told him about my problems and I asked him what I should do. He said: "Don't sweat the small stuff."

It hit me like a bomb. He suggested that I concentrate on doing a good job, doing what was right, and that if I wanted to worry at all to worry about big stuff, not small stuff. During the next few weeks, when the usual problems arose, I found that I could forestall the quick flare of temper and stop worrying about small stuff. I decided I would be concerned only with the big stuff.

Our family, our close friends, love, our health, our happiness, the helping of others, faith in God . . . these are the big stuff.

The auto breakdown? The red light that takes so long to change? The burnt toast? The charred steak that you ordered medium? The secretary who calls in sick on a busy day? The shipment that is late? Small stuff. Too small to spoil a day, an hour, even a moment. Even today, I wish I had learned that advice earlier. It would have saved me a lot of sweat.

For example, I had been working at the mill about two years when I became aware of a pain in my back. At first, it didn't bother me much, but then it kept getting worse and worse until I could hardly do any lifting on the job. Glenn Compton told me many times to go to a doctor. I thought doctors were for diseases and that chiropractors would know more about a back injury, so I started going to them. Despite their good efforts, the pain persisted.

One day, Glenn said: "George, I want you to see a back specialist."

I said: "I can't afford a specialist."

"Then I'll pay for it," he said. "You have got to find out what's wrong with you."

So we made an appointment with a specialist and I went for it. The doctor took X rays and did a lot of tests. His diagnosis: curvature of the spine. He said: "If you stay on the job you've got at the mill, your condition will grow progressively worse and you'll end up having problems and pain for the rest of your life. I strongly advise you to find some easier kind of work."

Easier said than done. I had no training for anything but unskilled labor. I thought of going to the personnel department at the mill and asking if they had a desk job on the management side, but I realized that even if they did I wouldn't know what to do at a desk except polish it. I talked things over with my mother. I talked things over with Glenn.

One day, Glenn said: "George, why don't you become a salesman of some kind? I've known you long enough to know that you can talk people in or out of anything you want. You'd be great as a salesman."

I thought that was a good idea. I liked people, I enjoyed meeting new people, and God knows I loved to talk. But what kind of a salesman? Selling what? I looked at the ads in the newspapers. Glenn and I drove around town, checking out the various companies we knew used salesmen. Nothing hit me right. Then one evening we passed the local office of a large insurance company. I said: "That's it, Glenn. I'll sell insurance. I should be good at that. Everybody needs insurance. I'll be a millionaire by the time I'm thirty."

The next day, I went there to apply for a job. Maybe I should have worn a suit, but I didn't own a suit, so I went in sports clothes, and that might have made me look too young. I filled out an application, I was interviewed by a man in his forties, and then I was told I would have to take a test. It was one of those performance tests that are supposed to reveal your hidden talents. There were hundreds of questions like: "Would you rather (a) attend an opera or (b) play basketball or (c) read a book aloud to a sick friend?" I'd never been to an opera, so I didn't know if I'd care for that; I hardly ever read a book to myself, let alone to anybody else, sick or well; but I loved playing basketball, so I chose (b). On and on I went through the test, wondering what it was all going to prove. Finally I finished and gave the test back to the man. He asked me to take a seat across the room while he went over my answers. For fifteen minutes, I watched him check my choices against an answer form he had, then add up points and fill in graphs. Then he called me back.

He said: "Mr. Shinn, I don't think there's anything we can do for you here. Your test shows that you have absolutely no sales abilities whatsoever. You'd certainly never be able to sell insurance."

That made me a little mad. Just out of my teens, I was surplus. I said: "Well, sir, I thank you for your time. I appreciate your honesty. But I must say it comes as a shock to be told at my age that I am washed up already. Sir, someday I hope to own my own insurance company. When you hear about it, look me up." I walked out.

I didn't realize it at the time but I was a prophet.

Glenn Compton and I continued to work at the mill, both of us on the night shift. There was a time when Glenn and I used to spend a few hours every evening carousing around town before going to work, but I didn't feel like carousing anymore. I stayed home all the time. My mother got worried. She said: "Junior, it used to bother me that you were running around too much, and now it bothers me that you stay home too much. Are you sick?"

"No. I'm all right."

"Is your back troubling you?"

"Not much."

"Are you doing the exercises the doctor gave you?"

Yes."

"Well, I just wish you wouldn't sit around and wilt like this."

That's what I was doing, wilting, in every way, and it wasn't like me. But I didn't know what to do about it.

A few evenings later, I was sitting by myself in the living room staring at the ceiling. My mother came in.

She said: "Junior, I want to talk to you about something."

"All right."

She said: "I know you're upset because you can't find a job that would be easier on your back. So I've been wondering about something. Do you think you could use some more education?"

"I know I could use a lot more education," I said, "but how am I going to get it?"

"Why don't you go to college?"

"Mother, you know we can't afford that. If I go to college, how are we going to live?"

"I wouldn't mind going back to work, Junior. In fact, I'd like it. You sleep half the day and you're gone all night. I'd like to have something to do with myself. We could work it out."

"Well, maybe we could, but there's something else. I'm getting a little too old to start out on four years of college."

"A lot of G.I.'s are doing it," she said, "many of them older than you are."

"You're right, I guess," I conceded. "But those boys must know what they want. I don't know what I want."

"You want a job that won't be too demanding on you physically, don't you?"

"Yes."

"Then it would have to be in some line of business, wouldn't it?"

"I guess so."

"Then why don't you go to a business college? That just takes two years. And you'll get some training for a job."

I said patiently: "Mother, business colleges are for girls who want to become secretaries."

"Not really," she said. "You know the Harrisons, in town? They own the department store."

"Yes, I know the Harrisons."

"Well, their boy is graduating from high school this year, and he is going to go to a business college over in Concord."

"He wants to become a secretary?"

"No, silly. He knows he will be taking over the business one of these days and he wants to learn something about business administration so that he knows what he's doing."

"That makes sense."

"It would make sense for you, too. You can't get an office job without some experience and you can't get experience without a job. Why don't you go to business college for a couple of years and learn something? The training would be the same as experience, wouldn't it?"

"I suppose so."

"Well?"

"I'll think about it, Mother."

The more I thought about it, the more I liked it. That night at work I discussed it with Glenn Compton, and he said: "It's a great idea. It could solve all your problems."

"Yeah," I said, "but there is the new problem of the tuition."

"Do you know how much it is?"

"No."

"Then maybe you don't have a problem. Check it out."

The next day, I drove over to Concord and had a talk with the director of the business college. I was surprised by the scope of the courses the school had to offer, so as we talked I became more and more interested. Then I asked about the tuition. It wasn't as bad as I figured. But when you have nothing in the bank, even a small tuition will look like a lot of money. I had a few weeks to make up my mind before the next quarter began. I told the director I would think about it and get back to him.

The only asset I had in the world was my car. By this time, I had replaced so many parts of the beat up old thing that it was practically a new car. I figured that if I could sell it for a good price I would have enough to pay the tuition for two or three quarters and still have enough left over to buy a cheaper car to use for commuting to the school. I decided I could worry about the rest of my tuition when the time came.

Even so, I still didn't make a definite decision. The decision evolved from an experience I had that New Year's Eve. Glenn and I had been invited to the same party. We got there around nine, and the party was just warming up when Glenn and I saw that we had about twenty minutes to get out to the mill and start working on the night shift. We both hated leaving the party, but we had to do it. It meant our jobs. So we left. We didn't have much to say to each other as we drove over to the mill. We didn't say much as we changed clothes and went to work. But I was doing a lot of thinking. I knew that I could stay on this job for the rest of my life if I wanted to, probably wearing a brace sooner or later. But what really bothered me was that I knew that, outside of my salary, I wasn't really getting anything out of my job. I had no complaints about the company. My complaint was with myself. I didn't want a job that would take me away from a party; I wanted a job I could take to a party. I didn't want a job that was part of my life; I wanted a job that would be my life. I wanted a job I could get excited about, and not just during working hours. I wanted to be somebody.

That night, I had been working about two hours, doing a lot of thinking, when I found myself near the foreman's office. I went in. He was working on some papers. He glanced up at me. I said: "I'm quitting."

He looked at me. "Oh? Why?"

"I'm going to college."

"Good for you. Sorry to lose you. Is this your two-week notice?"

"No sir. It's my good-bye. This is my last night."

"Okay."

I went back to work. About an hour later, Glenn came up to me, and he said: "I've just done something wild."

"What's that?"

"I just quit this job."

"You did? So did I."

We grinned at each other, feeling good. Glenn said: "Let's go back to the party." And we did.

A few days later, I took my car to a used car lot and sold it for a good price. By this time, I had invested so much in the car for new parts that it was practically brand new, so I got enough to buy a cheaper car, to pay the tuition at the business college for a couple of quarters, and to keep myself in pocket money during that time. I had no idea what was going to happen to me when the money ran out, but I decided I would worry about that later.

One thing I knew was that the next two years were going to be a struggle for me. But I was used to that. Being poor had forced my mother and me to struggle to make ends meet, even when the two of us were both working. Also schoolwork had always been a struggle for me. As long as I was getting my education free, this didn't bother me much; but now that I would be paying for my education I wanted to get my money's worth, and I knew that would be up to me.

Growing up on struggle, I came to the conclusion early in life that struggle was, perhaps, the only way that any-body got anywhere or anything. Everything, I found, had a price tag. When I was younger, the price tag always seemed to be a matter of money; but as I have grown older I have found that most of the time the price tag is something far greater, something called effort—great effort. How do you earn money? Through effort. Usually, the more effort you make, the more money you earn. But there are other price tags for success. For a college degree, the price is long hours and years of study. For a professional athlete, the price is long hours and years of practicing. A top-notch lawyer, a good mother, a productive farmer, an excellent doctor, a superb mechanic, a super salesman must all struggle to succeed and remain successful. Some people may not believe that we have to struggle to get into heaven but everybody agrees that we often have to put up a moral struggle to stay out of hell.

I believe that all living things are forced by nature to develop, grow, and become strong through resistance, and the more demanding the challenges are the greater the results can be. When I drive around North Carolina on short business trips, I often notice that the trees that stand alone in open spaces are always bigger and sturdier than the trees in the thick forests. I believe this happens because the trees out in the open are constantly struggling with all elements of the weather, not depending on other trees in the forest to protect them. It can be the same with each one of us who is willing to put up the struggle.

And there will be struggles if you want the good life. Anybody can exist. The government will put you on welfare and help you exist, but this could hardly be called living. To live, really live, you must be willing to pay the price—to struggle. Even if you have to struggle a long time, you must be willing to keep working at it. You must be willing to read, study, practice, make mistakes, get up and brush yourself off, and get going again.

Theodore Roosevelt once said: "It is not the critic who counts, not the man who points how the strong man stumbled, or where the doer of deeds could have done better. The credit belongs to the man who is actually in the arena, whose face is marred by dust and sweat and blood; who strives valiantly; who errs and comes short again and again; who knows the great enthusiasms, the great devotions, and spends himself in a worthy cause; who, at the best, knows in the end the triumph of high achievement; and who, at the worst, if he fails, at least fails while daring greatly, so that his place shall never be with those cold and timid souls who know neither victory or defeat."

Struggle, then, has a definite and useful purpose. Struggle can help you develop your mental and physical abilities, struggle can keep up your enthusiasm and inspire your imagination, struggle is a good way to build up your faith in yourself. Being willing to struggle, being willing to put forth your maximum effort at all times, is a shortcut to the strength and wisdom you need to solve the problems that come your way. And the life long habit of struggling can be the road to a long life.

It is a simple fact that success will not tolerate idleness. Just because you have struggled up the ladder to success doesn't mean that you can take the rest of your life off. Every successful person I know is always doing something, usually several things at once, and they thrive on it, even when it isn't a matter of making more money and even when they have retired. Going into retirement doesn't mean going into a vacuum, but I've seen a lot of people act like it. What happens if you tie your arm in a sling, taking your arm out of use and not moving it to achieve anything? The strength in your arm will soon wither and die. As with your arm, so will all the rest of you. The successful person keeps moving. I once knew a man who made his fortune and retired. He gave up the spirit of struggle because he believed it was no longer necessary. Over the next few years, he put on thirty-five pounds of excess weight, and he put his mind and body in a sling. He died of a heart attack at fifty-eight. Besides the loss to his family and friends, the man had been a loss to the community since the day he moved into the vacuum. There were so many organizations—civic, social, religious, business—

that could have used his know-how as a volunteer that he would have been busier than ever, happier than ever and, most likely, lived for a much longer time.

The Bible tells us that the suffering that can be part of struggling is expected of us as Christians. Peter 2:21-23 gives us Jesus Christ as our example. Jesus never sinned, He was never deceptive, He never answered back when insulted, and when He suffered He did not threaten to get even. He left His case in the hands of the Father, who always judges fairly.

Anybody in the business world knows that not all of us act that way. Every once in a while I run into people who try to avoid struggles by taking the line of least resistance. These are the people who don't honor agreements, who don't pay bills or loans, people who try to manipulate others for their own personal gain. When I meet such people I usually avoid them in time, which is about all you can do. It was from such people that I learned that the line of least resistance is what makes all rivers—and some men—crooked.

Disappointment can be a part of struggling, and so can discouragement. Disappointment can be a positive learning experience. Discouragement is negative and just drives you away from your goals. A good case in point is J. L. Brooks, a close friend and associate. When I met J.L. several years ago, he owned a private business school in Fayetteville, North Carolina. He was an excellent administrator and he loved his work. As I got to know him better, I found out that he was also a real scrapper. He had dropped out of high school and joined the Navy. While in the service, he earned his high school diploma. He also got married and became a father. After his discharge, he decided to go to college. This meant a struggle for four years, as he took all kinds of side jobs to support his family and pay for his education. Next came the struggle of raising money to buy the Fayetteville school. J.L.

survived both struggles successfully. And the school was successful for two or three years. Then the national economy went into a slump, and business schools were hit very hard. Unable to pay their tuition, students were dropping out left and right, and it was next to impossible to recruit new students. All of us in the business suffered, and J.L. came close to being wiped out. One day J.L. issued a check he knew he couldn't cover; but he knew he had some cash coming in at any moment, and his intention was to rush to the bank to make the deposit necessary for the check to clear. As often happens with cash coming in at any moment, it didn't. Two policemen went to his office with the check and offered him a choice between putting up the cash immediately or going to jail.

J.L. asked: "Am I entitled to a phone call?" The police said yes. J.L. called me.

When my secretary told me who was calling, I was so delighted that, not knowing his problem, I picked up the phone and greeted him with a big: "Hello, J.L., my friend, how are you doing?"

He paused, and then slowly and deliberately he said: "Marvelous."

"That's great," I said. "What can I do for you?"

"You can send me some money right away," he said, "'like by Western Union."

I knew he was having some problems, but I wasn't aware of the urgency. I asked: "How much?" He told me. I said: "No problem. It's on the way to you."

He said: "George, I'll get it back to you as soon as I can."

"Don't worry about it," I said. "I'm not." And I wasn't. I knew J.L. well enough to know that he was a good man in every sense of the word, and I also knew that he was simply a victim of the current crunch. At the time, I was trying to build up a network of business colleges, so J.L. joined our staff. Today J.L. is a successful top notch consultant, with an income any executive would respect.

Some time passed before I learned the full severity of J.L.'s problems on the day he called me, and I asked him how in the world he had managed to preserve his cool under such pressures. He said: "I trusted in the Lord and I never got discouraged."

Discouragement is usually self-induced. The going gets rough, nothing works out right, so chuck it. Two American Presidents had good advice for all of us faced with this situation. When asked what he thought was the main ingredient in success, Calvin Coolidge, never a man to waste words, just said: "Perseverance." And when Herbert Hoover was once asked what he did to lose the blues, he said: "I don't allow myself to get down in the dumps."

And James J. Corbett, the great prize fighter, had this to say:

"When your feet are so tired that you have to shuffle back to the center of the ring, fight one more round. When your arms are so tired that you can hardly lift your hands to come on guard, fight one more round. When your nose is bleeding and your eyes are black and you are so tired that you wish your opponent would crack you on the jaw and put you to sleep, fight one more round—remembering that the man who always fights one more round is never whipped."

Sometimes it is difficult to live by this attitude, especially when life seems to beating you to a pulp. I have been beaten to a pulp so often that at times I've wondered if I would ever solidify again. But you've got to be ready to take a beating once in a while if you want to develop the resilience that is essential to success. One more round? Okay. Perseverance? Definitely. Don't get down in the dumps? Well, at least not for long. Discouragement? Never. But the factor that is critical if you want to survive your struggles is J.L.'s special ingredient. Trust in the Lord.

I really enjoyed going to the business college. For me, this was a big switch. Previously, school meant next to nothing to me. I went to school simply because my friends were there; and if school held any appeal for me at all, it was in the area of sports. But at the business college I found myself applying myself to my studies like never before. Maybe the fact that I was now paying for my education gave it a special value to me. And maybe the fact that I was depending on the school to train me for a good job in the business world was the real inspiration. In any event, I stopped running around so much and spent more time at my books than I ever had in my life. And I enjoyed it.

Then came the bleak day when I discovered that I was broke. Some of my friends were working their way through college, but I didn't know if this was possible in a business school. To find out, one day I went to the director of the school, told him my problem, and I asked: "Is there any way I can pay my tuition by working it off around here?"

He thought about it for a moment, then said: "Yes, there is, as a matter of fact, but I don't think you'd take the job."

"What is it?"

"Well," he said, "we've got a woman who comes here once a week and does a pretty good job cleaning up the place, but I've been thinking of taking on another person to sort of tidy the school up on a daily basis. Sweep the floors. Empty the waste baskets. Clean the blackboards and the erasers. See that the rest rooms are in shape. Things like that. Be the janitor, in other words. That's the job."

"And I could pay my tuition doing it?"

"Yes."

"Great. I'll take it. Thanks a lot. I'll start today."

That settled my tuition problem. Now all I had to do was find a part-time job to keep myself in pocket money. Glenn Compton had gone to work in the supply room of a large bakery, and after I told him I was looking for a part-time job he was able to persuade his boss to take me on. I was paid on an hourly basis and I could choose my own hours, which left me plenty of time for my studies and kept me from becoming a financial burden on my mother. Actually, it wasn't much of a job. All I did was tote 100-pound bags of flour from a truck to the supply room and also tote the bags to the bakers when they needed some more to work with. It was practically the same job I had at the mill, except that the product was different and, not having to work long shifts, I didn't run the risk of aggravating my back condition.

One Friday after school, I wanted to attend an early evening basketball game, so I decided to put off my janitor chores until Saturday morning, when the school was closed. Saturday morning, I had just finished my job and changed back to my street clothes and I was just headed for the door when two teen-aged girls came in. I asked: "Can I help you?"

One girl said: "Do you work here?"

I said: "Yes." But I didn't say as what.

She said: "We're thinking about going to college and we would like to look around. Can you show us around here?"

"I sure can," I said. "Come on."

It took only a few minutes to show the girls around the classrooms which I had just made spotless. Then I took them into the office and started carefully explaining to them about the tuition and fees and the various types of study programs. I enjoyed doing it because I liked the place so much myself and was eager to talk about it to anybody who would listen. Before the girls left, they both enrolled and gave me checks as deposits on their tuition.

Monday morning, I gave the applications and the checks to the director of the school. He was amazed, and he asked me how I had done it. I said that I loved the school so much that it was easy for me to convey my excitement about the school to others, and that must have been what convinced the girls to sign up. The director thanked me, and I went to my classes.

Later that day, the two girls showed up at the school and they brought three friends along who were also interested in the school. They asked the receptionist if they could see Mr. Shinn. The receptionist thought about it, then said: "There must be some mistake. We don't have a Mr. Shinn working here."

"Of course you do," one girl said. "He showed us around Saturday and convinced us to enroll."

"Just a minute," the receptionist said. She went into the director's office and said: "Do we have a Mr. Shinn working here? There are some girls here who want to see him."

"What do they want?" the director asked.

"I'm not sure. One of the girls said Mr. Shinn enrolled them Saturday."

"That must be George Shinn," the director said. "I'll talk

to them." He got up and went out to the girls and asked: "Can I help you?"

One girl said: "We want to see Mr. Shinn. My three friends here are interested in enrolling and they want to talk to Mr. Shinn about it."

The director said: "George Shinn is a student here. He's also a student recruiter. He's in class now, so I'll be happy to answer your questions."

The girl shook her head. "We want to talk to Mr. Shinn or we'll just forget about the whole thing."

"Just a moment, please," the director said. He went upstairs to my classroom and summoned me out into the hall. He said: "There are some girls downstairs who are interested in the school, but they don't want to talk to anybody but you about it."

I said: "That must be the two girls who were here Saturday."

"Yes," he said, "and they've got three more girls with them who look like good prospects. Get down there and see if you can help them."

I went and talked to the girls. The director eavesdropped on the conversation, and after I enrolled them all, he said to me: "You did a terrific selling job, George."

Until then, I had never thought of personality as being a factor in selling. Now that I have spent several years at hiring people for all types of selling jobs I have come to the conclusion that personality can be even more important than experience. In fact, some of the best salesmen now with our company didn't have any selling experience at all when they were hired. I suppose that each one of us is a salesman in one way or another. We sell a product, we sell a service, we sell our convictions, we sell ourselves. For some, the personality required for good salesmanship of any kind comes naturally, but it can also be developed.

In my experience, the basis ingredient in a winning personality is liking people and letting them know it. Of course, you can't like everybody you meet, and it is human nature to like some people more than others. The fact remains that, in business and in life, the snarling, sarcastic, short-tempered person is his own worst enemy. I know. I've been there. Perhaps out of an impatience for success, I was a quick-tempered man for years, even with the people I liked best. I dated the same girl for eight years before we were able to get married, and now, looking back, I wonder how in the world she ever put up with me. Oddly enough, I learned the importance of letting people know that I liked them not from a human being but from a dog.

Shortly after we got married, Carolyn told me that she would like to have a couple of poodles in the house. That was all right with me. I was traveling a great deal and they would give Carolyn some company. We bought Ginger, a female, and Jolly, a male. Ginger was no problem, but Jolly was a nuisance from the minute he entered the house and took over. When he didn't have your undivided attention, he would bark his head off. I worried about the neighbors. Jolly was also very destructive, chewing up everything he could sink his teeth into. We had to keep remembering to shut closet doors and put things on high shelves. Carolyn and I fell in love with Myrtle Beach, South Carolina, the first time we saw it, and we enjoyed going there on weekends. We had to take the dogs along. With Jolly's incessant barking whenever we left the dogs alone, it didn't take us long to run out of motels that would let us come back.

As long as Carolyn would play with Jolly whenever he started acting up, he wasn't so bad; but when Carolyn became pregnant and didn't feel so playful anymore, Jolly went wild. I realized that the time had come for me to take control. Hollering at Jolly didn't accomplish anything except more noise, so I started walking around with a rolled up newspaper, and everytime Jolly so much as took a deep breath he got his little tail whacked. With my short temper, the daily newspapers were being rolled before they were being read. Carolyn warned me that the dog would get to hate me unless I cooled it.

Then Jolly acquired a habit that I couldn't help but find touching. No matter how often I'd hit him during the day, in the evening, when Carolyn and I would be sitting in the front room, reading or watching television or just chatting, Jolly would come into the room, jump up on my lap, lick my hand for a few minutes, and then fall to sleep. Once when he was licking my hand, Carolyn said: "See how much he loves you despite the way you treat him? Why don't you show your love for him?" I didn't say a word and I didn't make a move. I didn't want Jolly to find out that I was softening toward him. The newspaper remained always within reach.

Then Jolly acquired another habit, a bad habit. In the kitchen, Carolyn always put decorative place mats on the highly polished table, with fresh flowers in a bowl or vase. When Jolly got big enough, he would jump up on a chair and then jump up on the table and then chew up the mats and send the flowers smashing to the floor. It seemed impossible to break Jolly of this habit, mostly because he did it only when Carolyn and I were both out of the house. It was Carolyn who solved the problem. She found that by pulling the chairs too far away from the table for Jolly to make the leap, he wouldn't try. Pulling back the chairs became a family ritual whenever we knew that the dogs were going to be alone.

One Saturday morning, Carolyn left early to do some shopping and I had a meeting scheduled later at the office. As I was leaving, I noticed that one kitchen chair was too close to the table. The thought struck me to move it, but I had so much on my mind that I left without moving it. Shortly after noon, right in the middle of the meeting, the phone rang in the reception room, but I didn't answer it. A staff member who had come in to catch up on some work took the call, then came into my office.

He said: "George, it's Carolyn. She wants to talk to you."

Annoyed, I said: "Tell her I'll have to call her later."

He said: "George, it sounds like an emergency."

I went to the reception desk and picked up the phone and said: "Carolyn, I'm very busy right now." Then I heard her sobs.

"It's Jolly," she managed. "He's dead."

"He's dead?"

"Yes." She could hardly talk. "I just came home, and I found him dead on the kitchen floor. He must have taken a bad fall off the table."

It was like being shot. "Are you sure he's not just unconscious?"

"He's dead, George. I don't know how I went out without moving that chair."

"You didn't. I did. I'll be right home." All the way home, I prayed that the dog was just injured, just stunned. My heart burned inside me like molten steel.

I found Carolyn in the den, hysterical. I tried to calm her but I couldn't. I went out to the kitchen and saw Jolly on the floor. His neck appeared to be broken. His game over, Jolly had evidently lost his footing on the slippery table when he tried to jump back on the floor. I went back to the den and tried to calm Carolyn, but she was inconsolable.

I knew I would have to dispose of the body. I didn't want to bury it in the backyard because other dogs might find it. I called the vet and told him what had happened. He said to bring Jolly to him. I carried Jolly to my car and placed him on the front seat next to me. His eyes were still open. The vet's office was ten miles away, and I talked to that dog the whole way.

I said something to Jolly that I had never before said to a

male of any species. I told him that I loved him, and I asked him to forgive me for not ever showing him that I loved him. I also asked him to forgive me for being so selfish and self-centered that I wouldn't even take time to move the chair. As I talked to him, I found myself doing a lot of soul searching. I couldn't remember ever making much of a display of my affections for people. I wasn't coldhearted, but it didn't occur to me that I wasn't demonstrative, either. I knew I wanted to marry Carolyn when I first met her, but I didn't say anything about it to her for eight years, until I could finally afford to ask her. Also, I had friends I liked, I assumed they liked me, and we always had good times whenever circumstances brought us together. But, riding along and talking to Jolly, I suddenly realized that I had rarely, if ever, gone out of my way to establish a personal relationship with people who were not in some way involved with my business. I promised Jolly that I was going to change that. I vowed that, from then on, I was going to treat everybody as though today was the last day of their life—because it might be. And I learned that love has no value unless it is shared.

Not long after Jolly died, Carolyn gave birth to our son, Christopher, and Ginger gave birth to three pups fathered by Jolly. Fortunately, my son and the pups took after their mothers.

For me, liking people openly turned out to be a lot of fun. At work, I'd start each day making a tour of all the offices, exchanging greetings and brief conversations, and I'd end the day the same way. I began talking to strangers in restaurants, on planes, even on the street corners. I suppose some people thought I was an oddball, but I didn't care. I was finding out that most people are nice folks if you just give them the chance to show you; and to do that, you have to say the first word. I once discussed this with a friend of mine, and he told me a true story I think is pertinent.

Living in France about a hundred years ago was a girl who

was known as Thérèse de Lisieux. At fifteen, she felt that God wanted her to enter a Carmelite convent and become a cloistered nun under a vow of silence with the exception of a recreation hour each day. Her parents approved. In the same convent was a very old nun who had outlived her usefulness and couldn't bear it. During recreation hour, she complained and nagged constantly. Even during the silence, she was able to annoy people with her cranky personality. All of the other nuns disliked her and avoided her. But Thérèse decided she wouldn't be that way. She decided she would always treat the older nun with Christian love. During recreation, she was always pleasant and polite toward the old woman, chatting with her, seeing to it that she had a comfortable chair, bringing her tea and pastry. During the silence, Thérèse always deferred to the nun in obvious respect. This went on for week after week, and there was no noticeable change in the woman's behavior. She remained cantankerous with everybody. Then one day during recreation, when Thérèse brought her a second cup of tea, the old woman gave her a small smile and asked: "My dear, what is there about me that you find so attractive?" So you can't win 'em all. But you can try. As it turned out, it was Thérèse who later was canonized as a saint by the Catholic Church.

I found that being outgoing and letting people know that I liked them made me feel better inside. I had the usual worries and problems that any businessman has; but as long as I didn't brood on them or talk about them all the time, they didn't seem so serious. As far as other people knew, I didn't have a care in the world. And most of the time, I felt like it. Being cheerful can be a contagious habit, and once I learned that everybody else around me seemed to learn it, too. Life became more enjoyable, more fun.

Another thing I learned was that although it was easy for men to be flattering and affectionate with women it was difficult for a lot of men to be flattering and affectionate with other men. Jolly's death made me decide to put an end to that as far as I was concerned. From then on, when I noticed that a friend of mine was wearing a new suit that looked good on him, I told him. And when a relationship with a man matured to the point where it encompassed love, I told him that, too. C. L. Jenkins once told me about a visitor who spent several hours in the office and, as he was leaving, commented on the zeal and enthusiasm he had observed all over the place. He asked how come. Jenk told him: "Well, there is a lot of love around here."

In such an atmosphere, there is bound to be a lot of courtesy, pleasantness and kindness, and I think these are vital elements in personal advancement and company success. I've heard about a wealthy manufacturer who put on a pair of overalls every afternoon and joined his employees on the assembly line. One day he realized that he had to get to the bank before it closed, so he got into an old pick-up truck and made the trip as fast as he could, arriving just as a young clerk was shutting the door.

The clerk said: "Sorry. We're closed."

The man said: "Please let me in. I've got some important business to transact. It'll just take a minute."

The clerk looked at the old man in the soiled overalls, and he said: "Look, we're closed. If you want to do any business here, come back at nine o'clock in the morning." And he locked the door.

Promptly at nine the next morning, the manufacturer was back at the bank, and he said to the bank president: "If this bank can't stay open for one minute so that I can transact some important business, then I'm taking my business to a bank that will. Give me the forms necessary to close out my accounts here and transfer them to another bank."

The manufacturer was out of the bank at 9:01.

The clerk was out of the bank at 9:05—unemployed.

Looking back, I feel that an important turning point in my

life occurred that Saturday morning when I had the courtesy to show those two girls around the business college when it was closed. I didn't think of it as courtesy at the moment. I had the time and I was proud of the school. Besides, the girls were pretty.

After I enrolled those five girls the director said to me: "George, how would you like another job around here?"

"Instead of being the janitor? What's the job?"

"Recruiting. I'll pay you ten dollars for every new student you can recruit for the school, including these five."

"It's a deal."

Because the school was open all year and because freshman courses were offered each new quarter, this was a good opportunity for me. I didn't get rich off the job, but I gradually earned enough to cut down my hours at the bakery, eventually cutting them out. And I was having fun. I enjoyed having contact with teen-agers again. Many times I went to their homes to talk about the school with their parents, and I met some fine people. Because of my size and youthful appearance, some people asked me if I was recruiting for a kindergarten—all part of the razzing. It was fun.

My own two years at the school passed quickly and happily. But when I saw graduation coming, I faced the question that confronts all students: Where do I go from here? A month before graduation, I started reading the ads and writing letters of application. Nothing. I know something now that I didn't know then: the Lord prepares you for the ways in which He wants you to serve Him. What you are is God's gift to you; what you make of yourself is your gift to God.

About a week before graduation, the director of the school called me into his office. He asked: "Have you lined up a job yet, George?"

"No, sir, I haven't," I said.

"How'd you like to work here?"

"In the school?"

"Yes."

"As what?"

"A full-time recruiter."

I thought about it. "At ten dollars a head, I don't think I could make a living at it even if I recruited every new student you got."

"Oh, you'd be on a salary," he said, "a guarantee against commissions. Besides, the owners of this school have interests in a few other business colleges in North Carolina. You'd be working for them all."

That sounded better. "Well, I like the work," I admitted.

"Then why don't you give it a try and see how it goes?"

"All right, I will."

So I had a job. It turned out to be a lifetime job. It brought me a life that was better and bigger than I had ever dreamed I would have.

But there were also times when it was a life that was a living hell.

We didn't have any commencement exercises when I was graduated from the business college. There were too few of us for any kind of ceremony. We were just handed our diplomas and given congratulations, and that was it. We were then sent out into the world to make our fortunes. My world was right there at the school, and it was a long time before I saw anything like a fortune.

There were already recruiters working for the business colleges in which the owners of the Concord school had an interest, and these men were supposed to train me. Actually, I didn't need much training. I had already been recruiting for over a year. I loved the school and I enjoyed talking about it. And I was talking about it to my kind of people—country people. I understood them; I knew what was important to them; I was one of them. One day, I remember, an experienced recruiter and I went to a farm owned by the parents of a high school girl who had expressed interest in the college when she had been contacted at her school.

It was early evening when we got to the farm, and when the girl answered the door, she said: "We're just about to sit down to supper. Would you like to join us?"

For his own reasons, the recruiter said: "No, thanks. We'll wait in the car."

Being a country boy, I knew that when country people invite you for a meal, even on the spur of the moment, they are not just being polite. They really mean it. I said: "Well, I am hungry. I'd appreciate having supper with you if it's all right with your folks."

"Sure, it is," she said. "Come on in."

So the recruiter waited out in the car while I had a fine meal with some fine people. Mostly we talked about the school, and by the time we reached dessert I had the girl signed up. There were times, later in life, when I wished I didn't have my North Carolina accent, but in those early days of recruiting usually among country folks my accent would sometimes get so thick that I could hardly even understand myself.

Recruiting for four schools, I was kept busy and I was doing pretty good. It wasn't long before I was averaging around $600 a month, more than I ever thought I would earn. I didn't think I would ever go into any other business, and yet I wanted to be more a part of the business I was in. One day I went to one of the school owners and asked: "What are the chances of my buying a partnership in a school?"

"I don't know," he said. "I'll have to ask the partners who own it now. What's the matter? Don't you like recruiting?"

"Sure I do," I said, "or I wouldn't want to buy into the place. I just want to do more around here."

A few days later, the man called me into his office and told me that the owners had decided to let me buy into the business. The price they wanted was more than I had or could even raise, but the owners had taken this into consideration, too. They were willing to let me invest on the installment plan, holding back half of my earnings each month as a partial payment. I wasn't too crazy about this, but I knew there was no other way to go ahead with it.

Fortunately, I was still living at home with my mother, so I had few living expenses besides the upkeep of my car. My mother was worried about me. One night she asked me: "When are you going to get married?"

Because I didn't want to get too involved with any one girl, I was getting the reputation of being a fickle Romeo. I'd date a new girl a couple of times and then cool it for a few weeks before calling her again. I found that women didn't care for this sort of treatment, and it was lucky for me that I was working in three or four different towns and could blame business travels for my neglect. The lone exception to this reaction was a girl named Carolyn Smith who came to work at the Concord school as a secretary. She was pretty and nice and I liked her, so I dated her a few times. But then I felt the time had come for me to resume my "business travels." I wasn't fooling Carolyn a bit. Her job always let her know where I was. And when I felt it was safe to get back to her, she never displayed any resentment or impatience or displeasure, even though she knew I was dating other girls all along. Little did either of us know that our infrequent dates would go on for eight years, and it wasn't until we finally got married that I found out that Carolyn hadn't dated any other man in all those years. Maybe I married a saint.

I certainly married my job. I had said that I wanted to do more around the school. Before long, I was doing just about everything. Now that I had to be concerned about profits as well as my own salary, I wanted to save money at every turn. Besides continuing as a recruiter, I went back to work as the janitor so that we didn't have to pay somebody else to do the job. In those days, you didn't have to have a college degree to teach in a business college, so I became a teacher also. I taught every subject except shorthand, but I often read the dictation for shorthand examinations that were later graded by somebody who knew the language.

Our student population at the time was 80% female, and I knew why. Whenever I'd try to recruit a boy for the school, he'd ask: "What kind of an athletic program do you have?" We didn't have any. I decided to start one. With so few boys available, the only sport we could compete in was basketball. I made myself the coach. I loved basketball and, for my size, I was pretty good at it, but that didn't make me a good coach. I was soon sending out a team that was disgracing the school. There was only one thing to do.

The best athlete I knew personally was Glenn Compton. Having grown up with him, I'd watched him coach every kind of neighborhood team, and I knew he had the leadership and the skill to coach our basketball team. So I went to him and asked: "Glenn, how would you like to coach the basketball team at the business college?"

He lookd at me and winced. "I couldn't coach a girls' basketball team."

I said: "You take the job and I'll get the boys."

Glenn took the job, I'm sure, out of his love for sports but with little hope of achieving much, with so few boys as prospects for the team. But now I could tell prospects for the school that we had a real basketball team with a real coach, and the boys began to sign up. In a short time, Glenn put together a team that was beating the freshman-sophomore teams of some of the biggest colleges in the state.

The team also brought in a young man who was to become very important in my life. Jerry Daly, from New York State, had come South with the hope of getting an athletic scholarship at some small college, but it turned out that he lacked a few high school credits to get in anywhere. A coach who knew Glenn suggested that Jerry try us. I took one look at that tall, well-built kid, and I said: "You're in." And he was in—for life.

With time, I became more and more active in the business affairs of the school, and I didn't like what I was finding out. The school didn't have a certified public accountant. It didn't have a lawyer. There was no long-range growth plan. The whole thing was being run on a day-to-day, hit-and-miss basis. There had been some bad investments. I couldn't determine what the place was worth, whether it was making a profit or where the money was going. And this was a business college?

I did what I could to improve things. The building was old and so were the furnishings. We were still using desks that had ink wells. When Christmas vacation came, I bought a lot of paint in vivid colors—yellow, red, green—and I rented a spray gun and I painted all the desks and chairs myself to save the money. The place looked much better. But I hadn't done a good job. Some of the paint went on so thick that I thought it would never dry. When the students came back after the holidays, I didn't get the chance to warn them about the paint, and this meant I had to put out some more money to replace dresses and pants that suddenly had blotches of yellow and red and green.

I was putting in sixteen-hour days, seven days a week. I didn't mind that. I felt I had found my place in the business world, but as time passed I became increasingly uncertain that I was with the right organization. The owners were nice people and I liked them, but they had a number of different business interests, and I felt the schools should be getting more attention at the management level then they were. Besides the school at Concord, the owners had schools in Greensboro and Durham, plus part ownership in Raleigh and Fayetteville. J. L. Brooks was already at the school in Fayetteville, and I knew he was negotiating to buy it. In the meantime, owners of other business schools approached me with offers of jobs at much better salaries. I thought this over and realized that if I just changed jobs I would still be in the same boat—working for somebody else. I wanted a business of my own.

With this in mind, I went to the owners and stunned them by telling them that I wanted to buy their schools in Greensboro and Durham and their interest in the Raleigh school. On top of that, I made such an outrageous offer for the schools that they couldn't refuse.

I must have been out of my mind. I knew that the three schools were in trouble. Together, they didn't have a student population of two hundred. Although I had no firsthand knowledge of it, I was sure the schools were loaded with bills. I formed separate corporations to protect each school. I wanted very much to succeed. I was confident that I could turn things around. I had once told Jerry Daly when he was a student of mine that I was going to become a millionaire by the time I was thirty. The deadline was drawing close in terms of years, but in terms of income it was nowhere near close. But I was still confident.

My confidence shattered once I got a look at the bills. I couldn't believe it. Everything was a mess at all three schools. Companies we had to do business with wouldn't ship to us until our check to them had cleared, not even trusting us with C.O.D. Companies that hadn't been paid for a long time were sending us nasty letters and screaming on the phone. Lawyers were on the horizon.

I needed help of all kinds, and one person whose help I needed was Jerry Daly, just finishing up his own studies. I told him the truth about the whole situation, and he was very sympathetic, shaking his head and listening carefully. And then I threw him the zinger. I said: "Jerry, I want you to come and work with me."

He sank back in his chair. "Work with you? As what?"

"I'll need you for recruiting. We've got a lot of work to do."

"Yeah," he said, "but do we get paid for it?"

"At first we'll have to settle for the basic needs. We could save some money by sharing an apartment and doing our own laundry. What's important, Jerry, is paying the teachers so that we can keep the schools going and then paying the bills so that we can stay in business."

He asked: "How come it's 'we'?"

I looked him in the eye. "You go along with me on this, Jerry, and you will never regret it. I promise you that."

He shrugged. "I like North Carolina. I didn't want to go back to New York, anyway." We shook on it.

I had to shake with Glenn Compton, too, but it was a good-bye. With things as they were, I couldn't afford an athletic coach, so Glenn got a job with a large construction company. Whenever I was at Kannapolis, Glenn and I would double-date or just go somewhere by ourselves and have a good time.

Jerry and I worked our heads off. Just as we seemed to be getting a little ahead, there would be the teachers to pay and the creditors waiting at the door. It was like taking one step forward and then dropping two steps back. I'm sure I tried to borrow money from every bank in North Carolina, but with no luck. When I knew that I had a bank appointment the next morning, I'd spend the evening before rehearsing in front of a mirror, putting on the big smile until my face ached, making with the bubbly bravado until I reached the point where I wouldn't even have loaned myself money.

I began to feel the stress, turning into a eater, a regular drinker, a compulsive smoker. I went up to 180 pounds, which, on a man my height, is a Mr. Five-by-five asking for a heart attack. I didn't become an alcoholic, but a couple of nights a week I'd come home wasted and wonder in the morning how I got there. And I smoked so much that I was exhaling gray clouds even when I didn't have a burning cigarette in the same room. I became short-tempered, fluent in all the four-letter words used for chewing people out. I continued to date Carolyn from time to time during this period, and I'll never know how often she sat there, quiet, withdrawn, blushing, as I screamed at her for things she had nothing to do with and didn't even know about.

I needed help. Facing the fact that I had walked into this mess with my eyes open made me also face the fact that I wasn't as smart as I thought I was. I needed somebody to show me the way out. I had a friend who was a certified public accountant, and I called him and asked if he knew anybody like an efficiency expert who could give me some guidance. It so happened that he was part of a group of five men—three lawyers and two CPA's—who acted as a team in advising businesses. I could avail myself of their services for $500. It would be worth it.

An appointment was arranged, and I went over with all our accounting books and bills and earnings projections. For two hours, the five men and I talked everything out, examined every piece of paper, considered every turn in the road. Then I was asked to leave the room so that the five experts could discuss my position among themselves. Out in the reception room, I chain-smoked, my mind a blank, my heart full of fear. It didn't take them long.

When I was called back to the meeting, one of the lawyers said: "George, we have gone over everything thoroughly, and I'm afraid there's no way we can help you. Our recommendation is that you file for bankruptcy."

"I can't afford to file for bankruptcy," I said. "What about my earnings projections?"

He shook his head. "Those figures are based on the number of students you expect—hope, maybe—will register at your schools, and as such they are not a viable economic factor. You can't borrow money on daydreams."

"Thanks for your time," I said. I gathered up my papers and left.

Another lawyer, an older man, accompanied me to the elevator. As we waited, he put his hand on my shoulder and said: "George, why don't you just give up on these schools and get you a job working for someone else. You don't have a prayer. Not a prayer."

Not a prayer.

Those words haunted me for days.

Twice in my life now, I had been told, in effect, that I would never amount to anything, by the personnel man at the insurance company and now by five experts to whom I had paid $500 to be told I had wasted my money and their time. This is a dismal thing to be told. I knew I was not a daydreamer. My earnings projections had been based on the fact that high school graduations were to take place in about six weeks, and I had every intention of recruiting as though we were faced with war. Suddenly it didn't matter anymore. Even if I could pack the schools, I had been told that I was doomed. There was no sense in trying. The wind went out of me.

Not a prayer.

One afternoon I was driving along Interstate 85, on my way home to the apartment at the end of another hard day. I had called on several banks trying to raise payroll money for my staffs. After months of patience without getting paid, our employees had told me that this day was the last day. The banks all turned me down.

And the tires said the words over and over: "Not a prayer. Not a prayer. Not a prayer."

A thought struck me.

Prayer was all I had.

I hadn't been doing much praying lately. With so much work to do, there wasn't time for church on Sunday. There wasn't time to think about anything except how I was going to pay my bills.

But now a prayer was all I had.

I don't know which words passed through my mind and which words I said aloud, but I remember admitting for the first time in my life to being weak, and saying: "Lord, you know what a mess I'm in. I tried without you and failed. Nobody else will help me. I have tried everything and everybody except you. You are my only hope. Help me, dear God, to build myself and my businesses, and I will share with you. Please become my partner and the chairman of the board. You do the guiding and I'll do the work. Whatever happens to me, I'll share with you everything I have. I'll let the whole world know what you have done for me. Help me, Lord. Help me."

I became aware that I was crying. The taste of tears reached my mouth. I brushed the tears away, but they kept coming. I kept praying. Suddenly the front end of my car began to shimmy badly and I wondered if some rod had snapped. I didn't want to lose control of the car, so I pulled over and stopped. I kept crying. I kept praying.

I don't know how long I sat there. Gradually I got the feeling that I was coming out of a nightmare. I looked around, as though I had never been here before but knowing I had passed this spot many times. A sense of well being came over me. I knew I was still broke, that I had a lot of problems and that my companies had a lot of bills, but now this didn't sink me into the pit of depression where I had lived for months. I had the distinct feeling that I was not alone in that car, that I would never be alone again.

Jerry wasn't home when I got to the apartment, and I was glad. I was bursting to tell somebody what had happened in the car, but I didn't want anybody to think I had flipped my lid. I decided this was an experience I was going to have to live with by myself for a few days. But I knew I was going to tell people about it someday. My partnership with the Lord would be a bit phony if I made a secret out of it. I wanted to put it on record.

I hadn't slept well for weeks, worrying so much. That night I slept the sleep of the innocent. I awoke earlier than usual. I got right out of bed, went quickly across the room to the window, looked out at the world and said aloud: "Good morning, Lord!" And I didn't feel foolish. I felt great.

When I got to the office, the secretary was on the phone. She placed a hand on the mouthpiece and whispered: "It's the textbook publisher in Pittsburgh. He's having a fit. I told him you're out of town."

"Tell him I just got back. I'll talk to him."

She gave me the flipped-lid look.

On my way across my office to the telephone on the desk, I said softly: "Lord, you handle this." I picked up the phone and gave a hearty: "Good morning, my friend. How are you this fine day?"

"Not so fine," he said. He sounded like an undertaker.

"Why?" I asked, as though I didn't know. "What's the matter?"

"The matter, Mr. Shinn," he said, "is that I am looking at your bill, and you haven't sent us any payments in seven months."

"I realize that," I said. "I'll be sending you a check today."

"You will?"

"Yes, sir," I said, with a snap of a Marine.

"The full amount?"

It was about $2,000. "No, sir, but I'll send you what I can afford."

"Oh. Well, all right. Send something, anyway."

We hung up. I asked the secretary to bring in the checkbook. When I saw the balance, I knew that Mother Hubbard's cupboard had never been so bare. I said: "Send the Pittsburgh publisher a check for a dollar."

The flipped-lid look. "One dollar?"

"Yes," I said, biting my lip to suppress a smile at her astonishment. "And I'll be in all day. If any creditors call or come in, I'm here for them." She left the room slowly, in a daze. Alone, I had to laugh. And I said softly: "Lord, I hope you know what you're doing."

Three days later, I got another call from the Pittsburgh publisher, and he said: "Mr. Shinn, I got your check this morning. There must be something wrong."

I leaned upon the Lord. "What's wrong?"

"It's for one dollar."

"Oh, there's nothing wrong. The check is good. Go ahead and bank it."

There was a pause. Then he said: "Mr. Shinn, are you trying to be cute?"

I said: "No, sir. I've never been more sincere and more serious. The dollar is all I can afford right now. But I promise you that I will pay you in full. I will send you a check every week for as much as I can afford. And I also promise you that after we get things turned around down here I will be sending you a lot of business. Please be patient with me."

He said; "I think I've been patient enough. I'm considering turning this matter over to my lawyers."

"If you do that, you will only force me into bankruptcy, and then we will all lose everything. I want to do what's right. Please be patient."

He thought about it. "Well, okay, but not for long."

"It won't take long," I said. It was another prayer.

In the same way, with small checks and a promise to pay, I managed to calm down all the other creditors, knowing that I had only a prayer to go on.

I waited another week before I felt the time had come to let the people in the company know there had been a change in the organization. I asked the key people to come to the main office for a conference. That morning there were perhaps ten people at the meeting. Of them all, the only known Christian present was J. L. Brooks, who was still running a Fayetteville business school. The rest were all good people, but not demonstrably religious. Knowing the trouble I was in, some of them had offered to mortgage their homes to raise the money to keep the company going. I now felt that this would not be necessary.

As the group gathered, there was the banter that usually preceded such meetings. Then everybody sat down and looked at me, ready. I cleared my throat and said: "I think we should start this meeting off with a prayer." Flipped-lid looks around the table. I said: "Please bow your heads." Heads were bowed. I knew I was going to be nervous about this, so I had written out the paper the night before. Heads bowed, I took the prayer out of my pocket and read it. Nearing the end, I put the prayer away and went by memory to the Amen. A couple of people said Amen.

Then I said: "I want to tell you something that happened to me on Interstate 85 the other day." I told them. I tried to be as unemotional about the experience as I could, but I kept getting choked up. The account over, I said: "I want you all to know that you are no longer working for George Shinn. From now on, we are all working for the Lord."

Only J. L. seemed to be able to find his voice. He said softly but fervently: "Praise the Lord."

At the time, we had about 200 students in our four schools. Today we have over 5000. And we are consultants to all types of schools and colleges from coast to coast. Also, we are consultants to other types of businesses. We have gone into machine manufacturing, into insurance, into publishing, leasing of all types, gas and oil drilling, housing, and we are ready to go anywhere else the Lord may lead us.

With time, it became vividly clear to me that God had heard my prayer on the highway and was answering it in terms of providing guidance, guidance not only for me but for everybody on the staff. Morale was high, everybody was enthusiastic, and hard work became such a natural part of our lives that we were always looking for something more to do. Admittedly, we sometimes went into fields where we had no knowledge or experience; but we soon learned that we could acquire the knowledge in the process of acquiring the experience, and so we were always ready for any challenge, confident that the Lord was always with us as long as we were always with Him.

I hadn't realized that my life was on one big detour until I learned to look up. In fact, I recently had a specific experience in this regard. Carolyn and I had gone to Puerto Rico to attend a business convention of a wide variety of companies. I went expecting to take part in some rewarding discussions. Instead, the convention turned out to be an endless selling contest, with companies hustling their products every minute. I was disappointed; and as each day passed, I became increasingly depressed and bored. One night I couldn't sleep. Around 3 A.M., I got up and stepped out on the balcony of our hotel suite. I had learned to love the business world and I had met some wonderful people in it, but this crowd acted like a herd of wild animals on a stampede. Angry, I closed my eyes and shook my head, trying to escape my negative mood.

And then I looked up at the stars.

It was like suddenly finding myself in a church. The noises below seemed cut off. I was aware only of a beautiful and absorbing peace. If there really is a choir of angels, I'm sure I heard it at that moment, lifting my spirits and filling my heart with love. And I knew what had gone wrong for me. The pace at the convention had been so frantic that I hadn't had time to give the Lord much more thought than my good-morning greeting. I had been looking down—away from him for days. At this point in my life, I had grown so dependent on the Lord's guidance that if a day passed without asking Him for His blessing I would start to feel homesick. Standing there on that balcony in Puerto Rico, looking up at the stars, I could feel that the Lord was as close to me there and then as He had been in my car that afternoon on Interstate 85. I thanked Him for making me look up and realize that.

Later that morning I woke Carolyn and said, "Let's get out of this place." We had breakfast in the Virgin Islands.

This happened: one morning when I was alone in the office I got a call from Stan Huffman, a businessman who told me he had just read an article about me in a Charlotte paper in which the reporter wrote about how my faith had been the major factor in salvaging my company and my life. Stan said he felt the same way about what the Lord could do for people, and he said he'd like to have a visit with me. We made an appointment.

I liked the man on sight and we had a good talk. As it turned out, he was the head of a manufacturing company that turned out different types of machinery. He had come up with a new product and he needed some backing to promote it. I suggested that we discuss his idea with my associates, and I called the boys together in the conference room. As had become our custom, we began the meeting with a prayer. By the end of the meeting, the fellows recommended that we not only give Stan our backing but that, if possible, we buy into his company as partners. This would require the approval of his board, so we set up a meeting at S. E. Huffman Corporation in South Carolina.

At the meeting, the manufacturer said: "When I had a meeting at George Shinn's office the other day, we opened the discussion with a prayer. I liked that, and I think it's something this company should do. So if you will all bow your heads, I'll say a prayer."

We got on with the meeting, the merger was approved, and we returned to Raleigh.

Next day, Stan called me and said: "Something unpleasant happened here after you people left yesterday. The head of my sales department came into my office and said that he was quitting. I asked him why, and he said he has found out that he can't trust people who pray. He doesn't want to be part of the merged company."

I was stunned. "Is he really going to quit?"

"He already has."

"I'm sorry to hear that," I said. "I'm sure you've lost a good man who could have become a better one."

He was obviously a man of strong convictions, and they must have been convictions based on experience. The French have a saying: "Once bitten, twice shy." Maybe this man had been bitten once too often by people who start off with a prayer and end up with a shotgun, so I can understand his attitude. In Matthew 7:21, Jesus says: "Not everyone who says unto me, 'Lord, Lord,' shall enter the kingdom of heaven, but he that does the will of my Father which is in heaven." You can't have it plainer than that, and any businessman who thinks and acts otherwise is just kidding himself. When I was on the brink of bankruptcy, I wasn't saying "Lord, Lord" much, and when I did it was not in prayer but in frustration. After my experience on Interstate 85, I learned to say "Lord, Lord" before saying or doing anything else. And I was heard.

One thing to remember about guidance is that you've got to be expecting it or it won't get through to you. I have come to believe that God doesn't wait around to be asked for something. As long as you are with Him every minute, He is with you every minute, and the two-way communication is constant. Even the most insignificant event in your day deserves more than a passing glance.

One day, for example, I heard that Jack Jones, probably the most successful man in the business-school field, was traveling around North Carolina looking for some schools to buy. Besides being founder, president and chairman of the board of Jones College, a four-year college at Jacksonville, Florida, Jack Jones also operated a network of private schools all over Florida, and now he was evidently branching out. It would have been understandable, perhaps, if the news filled me with anger, resentment and fear. We already had enough competition without getting more of it from a man of Jack Jones's abilities, standards, experience, money and influence. But I didn't feel that way. In fact, when I first heard the news, my only thought was that I would like to meet the man and find out how he did it. I didn't make the effort for several days, until I became aware of a certain inner nudging, a kind of gut feeling, which I was beginning to recognize as guidance. I made contact with Jack Jones and we met.

He was an older man, in his sixties, warm, friendly, personable, outgoing. I liked him right away. Naturally, we talked mostly about the future in education. I told him I'd heard that he was in the market for some North Carolina schools and I gave him some names that might turn out to be good leads. He thanked me. I didn't want him to know what bad shape my own schools were in, but from time to time I'd bring up some problem that I had and he would tell me how he had once resolved something similar. He was totally unselfish with his experience and knowledge. I knew I was getting an education and I wished I could take notes.

At one point, he said: "Are you helping the veterans here in North Carolina?"

I knew that his schools had a terrific program for enrolling and training veterans so I asked what we could do to offer the same services.

"First, you get your school accredited and approved by all the necessary state and federal agencies. After that, you offer a superb product and then get busy doing what Congress intended for schools to do—inform our eligible veterans of their earned benefits, enroll them in school and educate them which will help them improve their life. The veteran will receive an educational allowance that will assist him in getting an education—a much deserved allowance for serving his country."

"Sounds like a fine program," I said.

"There can be a lot of work, especially when you are trying to upgrade your schools. Let me help you."

Not only was I getting an education, but I was getting a new lease on life.

Looking back, I know now that the meeting with Jack Jones was the turning point of my whole career, I firmly believe that the Lord brought the meeting about by persistently nudging me in Jack Jones's direction when I really didn't have a valid reason for going to him. But I had a lot to learn about my business and Jack Jones was the man who could teach me. That's exactly what happened. Not only did Jack give me important insights into his methods, but he assisted me and opened doors which I didn't even know existed. Jack Jones did eventually buy three business schools in North Carolina, including my old alma mater in Concord, and his competition didn't hurt us. In fact, he made us compete with ourselves, raising our standards and expanding our services, making our schools better than they might have become otherwise.

There is a grapevine in the business-school industry, just as there are grapevines everywhere else, and soon the word was going around that our schools were doing an amazing job. Other schools started making inquiries about whether we would take a look at their organizations and find out what they were doing wrong. That's how we became consultants. At first, some people thought we were crazy for aiding and abetting the competition, but I never felt that way about the competition. I have found competition to be good for a business, whatever it is. For example, our biggest and most thriving college is in Raleigh, where we have a great deal of competition from schools of all kinds, while a client we have in a town where there is no local competition is doing very good but not as well as the ones with competition. Moreover, I felt from the beginning that a successful business college was good for the whole industry. At one time, there was an attitude that business colleges were mostly for people who couldn't make the grade in a regular college. This attitude has definitely changed, certainly in North Carolina. These days, an accredited North Carolina business college must meet strict standards similar to our public colleges. This can only serve to raise the caliber of the schools and the caliber of the graduates and thus the caliber of young people going into the business world, with the business world being the ultimate beneficiary.

The first schools we advised were owned by friends of mine. When they asked what the consultation fee would be, I didn't know what to say. So, as I have been saying ever since to all kinds of schools and businesses, I said: "If we don't perform, you don't pay; but if our ideas do increase your revenue, our fee is based on a percentage." We reached a similar understanding with the students in our own schools, telling them: "If you decide that you don't like this place or that you feel you're not really getting anything out of it, just say so and we'll refund all unearned tuition and you can go some place else." That was, we realized, a risky way to do business; but we were now in partnership with the Lord and we wanted everyone to feel that they were being treated fairly.

A common attitude we found in many of the companies we examined was negativism. Perhaps the attitude was understandable in view of the financial problems, and yet negativism was usually at the heart of the overall problem. I had sieges of depression during the months of my own financial problems, but I never thought of giving up, of walking away, of quitting. True, if you're feeling depressed when you walk into a bank to ask for a loan, you can't expect the bankers to put much stock in you, and I'm sure that this happened to me many times. Even so, I never thought about getting out of the business: I was just struggling to find a way to work my way into the business. In my case, I was lucky to have a staff who wanted our company to succeed as much as I did, men and women who were willing to go week after week without a pay check, people who were ready to take out loans and mortgage their homes to keep the company afloat. Despite everything that was bad, there was one good thing we had: enthusiasm.

I know now that enthusiasm is a gift from God. In fact, the word itself is derived from a couple of Greek words meaning: "God-filled." Once we filled our company with enthusiasm, a tornado of optimism stormed through the whole organization. We had always been a peppery outfit, always joking with each other despite our woes, and this didn't change. But now that we had a higher purpose to work for than our own solvency, a new spirit of dedication hit us. We felt more worthwhile.

I once met a young woman who had made a similar discovery. She had wanted to become a school teacher, and she majored in education in college. For no apparent reason, she began to fall victim to a variety of diseases that puzzled the doctors. They couldn't figure out what was wrong with her, and yet they knew she was definitely ill. It occurred to someone that maybe the girl's problem was basically psychological, so she went to a mental hospital. She seemed to be improving when her father died, and she suffered a relapse. She became more depressed than before. She returned to the hospital and started taking shock treatments.

During her stay in the hospital, she was lying there one

day wondering what was wrong with her, what was missing from her life, why she was in such bad shape without any explainable reason. She glanced at her night table and saw a Bible which she hadn't noticed before. More out of boredom than anything else, she picked it up and began to read it. She told me: "The next morning I awoke and realized that God made this big, beautiful world, and He made everything in it. He also made me. And God don't make no junk. I realized that if I had turned myself into junk it was because I had never once considered for a moment that God wanted me to do good with my life."

When I met this young woman, she was in a seminary, on her way to becoming a minister and a missionary. She was in perfect health. And she was full of enthusiasm.

When our schools began to recruit veterans, we couldn't afford to take ads or publish brochures, so we had to do it the hard way. We got the names of every eligible veteran we could, and then it was a matter of calling and informing them of their educational opportunities with our institutions. Many were not aware of their benefits. What a joy it was being a small part of something that benefited so many people. Some of the veterans we met were from World War II, already set in their life styles, but a lot of them had teen-aged children who were thinking about college. We did everything possible to make them think about our colleges. The situation differed with younger veterans. Many of them were a few years older than the average college freshman and, despite the advantages of the G.I. Bill, they had put aside the idea of college and then starting on their careers at the bottom of the earning ladder. Understandably, they wanted to go to work and make some money so that they could get married, if they weren't already. The flexibility of our class schedules, plus the fact that we had night and weekend classes, appealed to them. They could hold down a job and still receive assistance to go to a college which, in a relatively short time, could prepare them for a more responsible position in life. They signed up.

Only another salesman—which was what I considered myself to be—could empathize with the joy of watching a business turn around and pick up speed. In our company, the joy was even greater because we knew our direction. Our goals were set and we were working toward them. Our enthusiasm grew so boundless that we worked for endless hours. We found that the more we tried to do for others the more we grew.

I have a friend in the Midwest who has made a fortune off doughnuts. That's right—doughnuts. He owns a highly successful chain of doughnut shops in his area. He told me once that he operates his business on the Extra Doughnut Principle. If other shops are selling doughnuts five for a dollar, he sells them six for a dollar. If the others competitively go up to six for a dollar, he goes up to seven. He says: "You make less on each doughnut this way, but you sell many more and win a lot of good will."

I have learned that this is a good principle to apply in just about any business. As our company went more and more into consulting, we observed that being penny-wise but pound-foolish was a common problem in many companies, and not just in terms of money. Efforts are wasted because not enough planning was done; projects fail because no alternatives were considered; the company goes down the drain because the gloomy attitudes in management pull the plug. The viewpoint has been too narrow and too negative. The little things have been overlooked.

For example, I always wear a suit, a white shirt and a tie to work. I do this because I never know how many strangers

I'm going to meet during the day, and I want to look my best for them. I feel that if you want to be an executive you should look like one. You only have one chance to make a good first impression and you should take advantage of it. Trivial though this may seem, it strikes me as a sign of respect for one's self, for one's co-workers and for one's job to be concerned about one's entire appearance. There is a sense of awareness in it.

So often, when several of us at our company go to another company on consultations, we find the executives of the other company dressed as though it made no difference. If an executive's job requires him to make contact with equipment or supplies that might soil his good clothes, it's all right for him to walk around in casual clothes occasionally. Otherwise, it isn't, if only out of respect. We never say anything about this, of course, but frequently we notice that after we keep showing up day after day in our white shirts, conservative suits and ties, the men from the other company start doing the same thing. This is a good sign. It shows the individual's new positive awareness about himself, and now we would have a creative attitude we could use as we worked together to solve the company's problems.

I will never try to force my convictions on other people, especially in the area of religion, but, with time, many of our people come to me either to tell me that they have made a commitment and joined a church of their choice or to ask me to pray for them while they try to improve their life.

Environment is bound to have an effect on people, and I have seen this happen in more ways than one. For example, as our work with veterans increased, we realized that we needed someone to head a new department for the program, someone who was a veteran himself and experienced in veteran affairs. It so happened that one of the veteran students at Rutledge College in South Carolina was having problems, so he wrote for advice to the National Association of Concerned Veterans, an organization dealing primarily with collegiate veterans. The president of the school then got a letter from R. R. Craig, then a regional coordinator for the organization, offering his assistance. They had a meeting. The president was very impressed with Craig and then advised me that Craig—who prefers to be called Butch—might be the man to head our veteran's department.

"There's just one thing, George," the president said. "This man's vocabulary is comprised mostly of four-letter words and he cusses up a storm all the time."

I said: "We hire people because of their capabilities. Many people in our organization have overcome greater problems than cussing. If he can handle the job, line up a meeting."

Butch was a sixteen-year Marine veteran when I met him. He is 100% disabled, his body still full of shrapnel, causing him great pain at times. His back was bothering him the day we met and he was on crutches, so I was prepared to hear him cuss up a blue streak. In fact, he hardly swore at all. We became friends and within a few months Butch was working in our organization.

It is customary at our company to start and end all staff meetings with a group prayer. Butch never joined us in prayer and he never said a word about his spiritual life. That was all right with me. He was doing a terrific job with the veterans.

One day Butch and I had to go to South Carolina on business, and I asked Jenk to come along. We went by company plane. On the way, we stopped off at Gastonia, North Carolina, where two ministers I knew had said they wanted to see me. One of them was a graduate of a seminary we were assisting and he was considering buying a building for his small congregation so he wanted my opinion of the building before he bought it. The other had made some improvements in his church building after a challenge was made when I spoke to his congregation and he wanted me to see that they met my challenge.

When we landed at Gastonia, I said to Butch: "We are going to spend an hour or so with a couple of local ministers. It's okay with me if you prefer to wait here at the plane."

He shrugged. "No, I would prefer to come along."

The two ministers picked us up at the airport and we drove to the building being considered for purchase. The price seemed fair, so I recommended the purchase. Then we went to the renovated church. New paneling, new carpet and a new organ gave the church an inspiring dignity and beauty. As we were about to leave, we decided to end our gathering with a prayer.

I whispered to Butch: "If you want to wait outside, it's okay." He shook his head. I said: "Then you'd better get ready to say a prayer because I think we're going around the room with it." He shrugged. Earlier, I had prepared the preachers about Butch and his strong use of four-letter words.

I said the first prayer just giving thanks for our many blessings. Then one of the preachers prayed, and he simply asked God to show Butch how he could grow if he would accept His guidance. The second preacher also included Butch in his prayer.

Then it was Butch's turn. I looked at him. Tears were streaming down his face. When he could speak, he said: "Lord, I give you my life. Come into my heart and make me a better man. Help me to grow." I was deeply touched.

After that, I noticed that his language improved and that he started to pray at the office sessions.

Time passed. One day I had to catch a plane, but first I had to go over to Durham for a brief meeting and I needed someone to give me a lift. Butch was the only person in the office who was available. After the Durham meeting, we headed for the airport, and I saw that we had time for lunch. We stopped off at a local cafeteria where about half of the customers were blue-collar workers. When we were settled at our table, I noticed that Butch had gone kind of quiet, which was unusual for this talkative man. He had tears in his eyes and when I asked him what was wrong Butch said, "George I am so happy because you taught me to love the Lord and I want you to know that I love you helping me become a better man. I am so happy that I want the whole world to know. As a matter of fact I am going to start telling the whole world right now."

To my amazement, he stood up and in a very loud voice called out: "I love the Lord." He sat down. The quiet remained for a moment or two; then people resumed their conversations.

To my amazement, he stood up again and in the same loud voice said: "I also want you to know that I love George Shinn, too." He sat down. Quiet for a few moments. Then conversations again.

I said: "Please calm down before they throw us out."

A few minutes later, some men at a nearby table finished their lunch, and as they were leaving one of them came to our table, extending his right hand to Butch, and he said: "That was a fine thing you did. I love the Lord, too."

Butch rose and shook the hand and said: "I'm glad to know that."

The man said: "But there is one thing I've been wondering about."

"What's that?"

"Who is George Shinn?"

During those months of business turmoil, my mother called me one morning, and she said: "Junior, Glenn Compton was killed this morning. He was working at Lake Norman and a large concrete door weighing several tons broke off from its holdings and fell on him. He was killed instantly."

"Oh no."

"It's a terrible thing, Junior. The whole town's upset. Everybody liked Glenn."

"I know. I loved him."

"Are you coming home for the funeral?"

"Yes. I'll leave right away. See you as soon as I can, Mother."

Seeing Glenn Compton in his coffin had a profound effect on me. He had just recently visited Raleigh and we laughed and discussed old times and our future. Now he was dead. Looking at him, I knew that if my business hadn't been so bad, Glenn wouldn't have been working at the construction company—he would have been working for our organization. The thought depressed me and made me feel guilty, and I had a hard time shaking it off.

I could not remember when I had last given death a thought. Now I realized that, like Glenn, I could die at any moment. For years, I'd had very little to do with the Lord, so little that it did not occur to me to turn to Him at this moment. I just felt very empty, very alone, very unsure.

Glenn died about four months before my experience on Interstate 85, and at times I have wondered if Glenn had anything to do with it. Like me, he had been a churchgoer in his youth; like me, he drifted away from religion as he grew older. But I believe that God puts into each one of us a seed of faith and then He leaves it to us to cultivate it. It is never too late. In this regard, I often think of Dismas, the repentant thief, who was crucified with Jesus Christ and who asked for salvation with his dying breath. He got it. I'm sure that Glenn got it. Also, I believe the prayers we say for each other are answered whether the prayers are said in this world or the next world. I know that Glenn loved me. If he didn't know what bad shape I was in while he was alive, he certainly got a clear picture from his vantage ground in Heaven. So it might have been Glenn who nudged me toward prayer when other people were saying I didn't have one.

That prayer was the beginning of the cultivation of my faith. And the cultivation hasn't stopped since. I just wish I had started earlier.

Another man of lifelong faith is my friend and associate C. L. Jenkins. When Jenk was in his forties, he was driving in a rainstorm one night when his car skidded off the road and rolled over several times. Jenk's back was broken, and the doctors told his family that he would probably be dead before morning. He wasn't. In his fifties, he had a severe heart attack, again the doctors warning the family that the end was near. Jenk recovered. In his sixties, the doctors told Jenk he had cancer, but he survived that, too. Also in his sixties, Jenk suffered the pain of watching his beloved wife die slowly of cancer over a two-year period. As I was getting to know Jenk and learning more and more about him, I commented one day that he must be some kind of a man to be able to go through such ordeals and still have such a positive attitude.

He said: "If I didn't have the faith in God that I do, I wouldn't be here today. I have always believed that the Lord has a job for me to do and that He's not going to let me move in with Him until I do it."

Jenk is in his seventies now and is as full of the real zest of life as anybody in our organization.

When the Lord's blessing started and some profits began to come in, I immediately took up tithing both myself and the different companies I owned. I also got married. Carolyn and I decided to have our marriage ceremony on April Fools' Day because we didn't think people would believe us after dating for eight years. We settled in Raleigh.

After a short time, we felt we ought to join a church. For the next few months, we went to a different church every Sunday morning. Carolyn was accustomed to the more sedate preachers, but I wanted somebody with a little fire in him, so we kept circulating week after week. Then one Sunday morning we went to Hayes Barton Baptist Church, where the pastor was Dr. T. L. Cashwell, Jr., and we found our man. Later in the week, we went back to the church and joined, and after that we attended regularly when I was not speaking at another church. Jenk, a widower then, was very active, and that's how we came to know him. Retired, Jenk had been successful in the auto-parts business, and he was looking around for things to keep himself busy.

As 1973 unfolded, our accountants called and told me the unbelievable amount of earnings we had made. I was amazed but happy. Now I could keep my commitment that I would share with God whatever He sent my way. Up to this point, my tithing money went to churches or church-oriented projects I heard were in need of finances, but it was all hit-and-miss. An advisor told me: "If you're going to keep giving all this money away, you'd better set up some kind of organization to make sure that you're distributing it wisely."

"I'm all for organization," I said. "What do you suggest?"

"Why don't you set up some kind of a foundation to supervise your donations and find a good man to run the whole thing for you?"

"Where do I find a man like that?"

He said: "You're the business pro—you find one. Meanwhile, see a lawyer and get that foundation in the works."

I saw the lawyer and I started looking for someone to run the foundation.

Blessings were flowing to me and now I must channel them back to help others. I phoned Dr. Cashwell and told him that I'd appreciate it if he would come by my office whenever it was convenient for him. We made an appointment.

When we were together, I said: "Dr. Cashwell, I have been greatly blessed beyond all my expectations. I haven't given to the Lord regularly, so I feel I have a lot of catching up to do. I want to give this to Him through you to use in any way that you feel is best." I handed him a check for $10,000.

He was amazed. He said: "In twenty years in the ministry, this is the largest single donation that I have received."

"I'm surprised," I said. "You have a lot of successful people in your congregation. If the church ever gets in a financial bind, I hope you will let me know."

He said: "We have a generous congregation, and each member has a duty to support his church. If I ever see that the church needs some extra money for some project, I'll announce it from the pulpit and let each person do what he can."

I nodded. "You're the boss."

I wasn't having any luck finding some person or some group for guidance for the foundation. I knew we would have to start small, so some person or some group part-time would be good enough, but there didn't seem to be anybody around. I talked to Dr. Cashwell about it and asked him to keep me in mind.

A couple of weeks later, Dr. Cashwell called me and said he had someone he wanted me to meet, so we set up a lunch date. The person was C. L. Jenkins. Actually I had met Jenk before, at the church, but we were part of a large crowd and didn't have a chance to talk. As we talked at lunch, I found myself liking the man. He was bright, he had a fine sense of humor, and he had a sparkle in his eyes that let you know he was full of enthusiasm. I told him about how I wanted the foundation to help people to serve God, he nodded repeatedly, understanding, agreeing, and I was sure I had found my man. Actually, it wasn't I who found him—God had found him, but I didn't know that for a long time, until Jenk finally told me his story:

"After my wife died and I retired, I turned into a golf lover, spending most of my time traveling all over the South playing different golf courses. I had just finished three weeks in Alabama and decided to go home for a few days. On the way, I stopped off to spend the night with my brother in Charlotte. Next morning, I headed for Raleigh.

"I was on the road about thirty minutes when suddenly I felt terrible. In the past when this happened, I just prayed and the Lord always gave me guidance. But this time it didn't work. I kept asking, but I wasn't getting any answers. At one point, I discovered that I had driven thirty-five miles without being aware of an inch of it. I realized this was dangerous and I tried to pay attention to the road, but I couldn't escape the feeling that the Lord was trying to lead me.

"I always travel with a few books to read. At this point, I had about a third of one book to finish. When I got home, I decided to finish the book before unpacking. I sat there for fifteen minutes staring at the book before I realized that I hadn't turned a page. I had the feeling that I wasn't alone and I kept glancing around the room.

"I gave up on the book and turned on the television set. It was a movie: a man was sitting at the hospital bedside of his wife, who was dying of cancer. This made me think of my wife, who had died of cancer, and I started to cry, crying harder than I did when Mary died.

"I felt so helpless. I turned off the set and went to the bedroom to go to bed. Then I knelt at the side of the bed, and I prayed: 'Lord, I don't know what's going on. Please tell me. I know you're trying to get through to me but I can't get the message. What should I do? Give me some guidance. Open a door. Here I am in my old age. Take me. Use me. I'll go the way you want.' Then I turned off the light and went to sleep, and I slept like a baby.

"In the morning, I felt an urge to call Dr. Cashwell, something I rarely did midweek mornings because I knew how busy he was. I greeted him with: 'Hi, there, T.L. It's Jenk. I'm back in town.'

"He asked: 'Where've you been?'

" 'On another golf trip,' I said.

" 'You're wasting your life,' he said. 'Get up here.'

"I went there. We visited about a half-hour. I thought he had something to say to me, but when it seemed he didn't, I felt I shouldn't take anymore of his time. I got up. Impulsively I said: 'T.L., find me something to do. I really want to do something with my life. Maybe I can do volunteer work in a hospital, helping out with older people. Maybe there's a family around that needs some help. Find me something.'

"He said: 'Sit down.' I sat. He asked: 'Are you willing to come out of retirement?'

"I said: 'No.'

"He asked: 'Are you willing to meet a fine young man who is a good Christian and who is looking for somebody to direct his foundation for doing good works for the Lord? It would only be a part-time job.'

"I said: 'Yes.' I didn't want the job, but I wanted to meet that sort of man.

"A few days later, Dr. Cashwell and I had lunch with George Shinn. I recalled meeting George several months before at the church. As I sat there listening to George talk about his convictions, his principles, his goals and his love of the Lord, I got the growing feeling in my heart that I was going to come out of retirement, at least part-time."

Of course, I didn't know all this about Jenk at that lunch, but I got the gut feeling that this experience was guidance. I offered him the job.

Jenk smiled and said: "When do I start?"

It was easy to find churches, church groups and church individuals who needed money. The difficulty was deciding which we could help within the limits of our charter. The decisions became Jenk's job. He started traveling all over the country a great deal, checking out requests that came to us and needs we heard about, developing an excellent sense of judgment of people and situations. Jenk found that many seminary and Bible college students were having financial problems because many of them could not afford to attend college. In a short time, we had 150 worthy students training for careers in Christian living. When I think of all the good these people will be accomplishing in the years ahead, I realize that the Lord knew what He was doing when He answered that prayer of mine.

A businessman once said to me: "I pray and pray and my business keeps failing. Why?"

I asked: "Is anybody else in the organization praying for the company?"

He thought about it. "Not that I know. I'm pretty sure I'm the only one."

"There is your problem," I said. "A company is a group of people working together to produce a product or a service. A company isn't just one person; it's a group. Well, if your people are willing to work together, they ought to be willing to pray together. Start calling your people together for prayer sessions. Do it regularly."

"Oh, I couldn't do that," he said. "We've got people from too many different denominations in our company."

I said: "What's that got to do with it? They all pray to the same God, don't they?"

"But what do I do about the people who aren't believers in the first place?"

"Make believers out of them. The rest of you say your prayers, and when the non-believers see how the Lord is guiding you they will change and come around. I've seen this happen in our own company. It can happen in yours."

He did some more thinking. "Then God just takes over?"

I said: "Not really. God will guide you if you and your people get up off your cans and do the work."

I was able to give him a recent example. We needed a bigger building for one of our schools because of increased enrollment, projected by one of our recruiters—so a couple of us looked around the town until we saw a building that we liked. We got in touch with the owner and we began negotiations. We wanted the building and we wanted it fast, so we didn't intend to put up much of a fight. The transaction shouldn't have taken more than a week or two. But things kept going wrong on both sides. We'd find out that there were some more forms to fill out. Twice we scheduled the closing, but something important would force me to fly to some other part of the country. The owner dropped his price, which made the deal even more attractive, but it just didn't seem possible to wrap the deal up. One morning, our people had a special prayer session about the transaction, and during the discussion that followed we agreed that someone from our company should take a good look at the investment so that we could make the right decision. We continued to run into roadblocks. Our new semester was to start soon and if we didn't have more facilities we would have to turn down approximately 200 new students. The fall semester came and we did not have enough room for the projected 500 new students we were expecting. But we started only 300. A young recruiter had lied about the number he had enrolled, he reported about 200 more than he actually had enrolled. It cost us a lot of time and money and it cost him his job. Isn't it funny how our problem could have compounded if we had purchased the expensive building? A board member said to me: "It is unbelievable how God looks after us. We would have made a big mistake on this deal, but He knew best and prevented us from having something we thought we needed."

That is answered prayer, too.

Glenn Compton's death made me more aware of life, especially my own life and the condition of it. With the exception of an occasional cold and a persistent nasal problem, my health was generally good.

After taking my annual medical check up, the doctor said: "Well, you're overweight—that's for sure. I suggest you try to take off some weight."

"All right."

"Your cholesterol is high. Cutting down your food intake

will help that, and I'll give you a list of foods to avoid. Remember, your family has a history of heart attacks."

"What about my nasal problem?"

"I'll give you a prescription for a nose spray."

Although I readily accepted the doctor's orders, I knew I was in trouble before the words were out of my mouth. The first think I did when I got out of his office was light a cigarette. Like most heavy smokers—I was up to two packs a day—I usually lit up without thinking about it, without really wanting a cigarette. I was at my car before I realized what I was doing and I threw the butt away. I knew this was going to be rough. As for the drinking, I hadn't reached the point where I had to have a drink with breakfast, nor was I nipping in the office. But I always had a couple of beers after work and a few drinks at night. At a party, I could keep up with the biggest boozer present. But I didn't think I had a drinking problem until I tried to completely quit.

But the big problem, I knew, would be the food. I had become a compulsive eater. From the moment I opened my eyes until I fell asleep at night, an assortment of food was rarely beyond my reach. I had snacks on the night table, snacks at the television set, snacks in my car, snacks on my desk. I used to tell people that I snacked so much because I didn't always have time for regular meals, but that wasn't true. I seldom went a day without three meals, big ones, heavy on the rich desserts. I had to face the fact that I had become a glutton. Maybe business worries and frustrations did it to me, but if this was the explanation it was also the excuse.

Like the average prisoner of habit, I told myself that I couldn't break my habits cold turkey. I would have to taper off. I told everybody that I knew what I was trying to accomplish and asked them to stop me if they caught me slipping. It was hell. I slipped, of course. There was the cigarette in the men's room, the drink while out on the town, the cone of ice cream gulped in my car. I was suffering every minute.

The suffering stopped the morning I stepped on the scale and found that I had lost ten pounds. I had never felt so triumphant. After that, the torment became a lark. By the end of the month, I had lost thirty-three pounds, I hadn't had a cigarette in almost three weeks or a drink in over two.

But the nasal problem had been persisting for five years.

Sometimes the headache pains would put me close to tears. The nose spray the doctor had prescribed was only mildly and briefly effective. I had to keep using it for five years and by that time it wasn't much help at all. My short temper worsened; I was screaming at everybody, even Carolyn and my mother. Rarely did I get a full night's sleep. Wherever I went, I asked people if they knew a specialist who could help me.

The doctor had warned me not to use the new nose spray too much because of its strength. But the relief it gave me at first was so wonderful that I never hesitated to use it. In time, I was using the spray every few hours. I had them everywhere—in my pocket, in my briefcase, in my desk, in my car, all over the house, and I had no idea what a dependence I was developing on them. Despite the relief they usually provided, I knew they were not improving my condition, and that's what I was mostly concerned about.

I heard about a doctor at an important medical center who was a specialist in nose afflictions and I made an appointment with him. He turned out to be a much younger man that I expected, and it was easier for me to talk to him. I told him the whole story. He listened without showing any reaction at all. Then he examined my nasal passages. Then he sat down and crossed his legs and looked at me somberly and I got myself ready for the worst.

He said: "George, the membranes in your nasal passages have become dependent on the nose spray. They cannot function on their own. They are like jelly. Without the spray, they stop up your nose and you start getting the headaches. When you use the spray, you dissolve the substance enough to give you some relief. The problem is that I can't do anything about your basic ailment as long as you keep using that spray."

I asked: "What should I do?"

"You've got to stop using the spray."

"I'll stop," I said.

He shook his head, as though I had said something that was impossible. He asked: "Do you smoke?"

"Not anymore."

"How much were you up to?"

"Two packs a day."

"Why did you quit?"

"For health reasons."

"Was it rough?"

"It was hell."

"Well," he said, "that was child's play compared to what you're going to go through if you try to stop using that spray. A lot of people wouldn't be able to do it. If you were an older man, I wouldn't even recommend that you try. It will be the ordeal of your life."

I thought of the woman who realized one day that God didn't make no junk. I said: "I'll stop using it."

He nodded in a patient but not believing way. "All right," he said. "When you do, get back to me and we'll see what we can do for you."

Before I got to my car, I had need of the spray, but I refused to use it. By the time I got back to the office, I had a splitting headache. And that was only the beginning.

I had no idea that a human could go through such an experience. For the next three days, I was in ceaseless torment. Every part of me ached, as though I was being squeezed in a vise, I couldn't lie down, I couldn't sit down, I couldn't stand the weight of my clothes on my body. One minute I felt on fire; the next minute I was an iceberg. I was constantly sick to my stomach. I did not sleep at all.

All I had was the Lord. I kept saying His name over and over again—the only prayer in my heart. The pain was still there, but at least I could bear it.

On the third evening, I was so exhausted that, after Carolyn went to bed, I fell asleep sitting up in a chair while pretending to be watching television. A humming sound awoke me around two in the morning. I saw that the television screen was blank. I had a slight pain in my back. When I got up to turn off the TV, the pain stopped. I stood there for a moment, waiting for the pain to attack, but nothing happened. I felt almost normal. I turned off the lights and went up to bed.

Usually I beat the alarm clock in the morning, but this morning it buzzed for so long that Carolyn nudged me and told me to turn it off. Apprehensively, I got up. No pain. No sickness. I turned off the clock and went to the window and looked out at the world. I whispered: "Good morning, Lord. Is it over?" The answer came in the sense of euphoria that filled me. I found myself grinning, something I hadn't done for a few days.

I still wasn't sure. All day, part of my mind was in fear, ready for a return of the hell. Nothing happened. I waited until the next morning before calling the doctor, and when I had him on the line I said: "Okay, what do we do now?"

He asked: "Is it over?"

I said: "Yes."

"This is amazing," the doctor said. "I never heard of anything like it before. George, you must be a man of strong faith."

"If I wasn't before," I said, "I am now. I couldn't have done this on my own."

And I couldn't. I believe now that nobody can achieve anything of value without the Lord. Like everyone, I've met men and women who appear to have become successful without any help from the Lord, but I've noticed that sooner or later life seems to backfire for these people. They make a mistake and lose a lot of money, maybe even their business. Their partnerships go sour. Their marriage falls apart. One of their kids goes bad. Certainly I don't believe that these things happen because God is punishing anybody—I believe they happen because the individuals themselves are not shored up by the Lord's blessings, which they can have just for the asking.

The proof is in the Bible. In John 15:7, Jesus says: "If you abide in me and my words abide in you, ask whatever you will and it shall be done for you." And in Matthew 21:22, Jesus says: "And whatever you ask in prayer, you will receive, if you have faith." And in his 33:3, the Prophet Jeremiah records that God told him: "Call to me and I will answer you and will tell you great and hidden things which you have not known." What more does anybody need?

I gave a talk one day to a men's club and during the question-and-answer period, one man asked: "How does a person get to love the Lord?"

I said: "How does a person get to love anybody? Through communicating, talking to one another, spending time together, working and playing together, being near each other in person or by phone or letter or just in thought. The love of the Lord has to be a living and growing thing and you've got to work on it on a daily basis, the same way you got your wife to marry you."

Then his tone got a little sarcastic as he asked: "So you and the Lord are communicating with each other everyday?"

"Absolutely," I said. "I communicate with the Lord when I think about Him, when I pray to Him, when I talk things over with Him, when I read the Bible, when I try to make decisions the way He would. The Lord communicates with me by sending me guidance and blessings."

"You get guidance?"

"Yes, I do. Sometimes it's in the form of a new idea. Sometimes it's a thought that hits me in the middle of the night, and I jot it down. Sometimes it's suddenly seeing the answer to a problem that's been bugging me. Sometimes it's what somebody else says or does. Sometimes it's in the form of somebody new the Lord sends into my life. Whatever it is, I know it is guidance coming from the Lord because there is no other explanation for it."

He asked: "Have you got any evidence of that?"

"I sure do," I said. "Everything that I have accomplished has been beyond my own abilities. For years, I tried on my own and failed. Now with His guidance I have become a better person, and He will continue to guide me if I only, first, ask, second, have faith, and, third, act. That means putting all of my faith into action. If you apply that simple but powerful formula, you will succeed—you cannot fail. What more evidence do you want?"

10

While in school I had never been much of a book reader, but I was beginning to spend more and more time reading motivational and self improvement books from authors like Dr. Norman Vincent Peale, W. Clement Stone and Napoleon Hill.

I was impressed with Dr. Peale. His direct style of writing, his warmth, his sense of humor all appealed to me, and what he had to say about bringing the Lord into every aspect of your life certainly was on target with me. He seemed to know all the important people in the world and told inspiring stories about what faith had done for them. I'm sure I read *The Power of Positive Thinking* a dozen times, and each time I got something new out of it.

One thing I gained from my reading was the habit of always having paper and pencil handy to jot down any ideas or thoughts that might come to me. I even kept a pad of paper and a pencil on my night table, just in case an idea would come to me during the night. It so happened that I started waking up at night with something on my mind, and I'd jot down a few notes to remind myself of it in the morning. Sometimes I'd fall back into such a deep sleep that when I awoke in the morning I'd forget about the notes and wouldn't know about them until I looked at the pad.

Carolyn and I had been married only a few months when one morning she said: "George, something happened during the night that I'm a little concerned about. I awoke around three o'clock this morning and looked over at you. You were lying on your stomach and you had that pad of paper on the bed in front of you and you were writing away like crazy—in the dark."

"I was? Good gracious."

"I asked you what you were doing and you said for me to shut up that you would have it worked out in a minute."

"Is that right? Well, I don't remember it."

I also started keeping paper and pencil on the dashboard of my car, and I trained myself to be able to make a few notes without taking my eyes off the road. And always at my side was a casette recorder, just in case I wanted to go into detail about something. Usually I didn't play the car radio when I was alone on a long trip. I liked the silence and the privacy which gave me the opportunity to give thought to any decisions I had facing me. But one night I did play the radio.

I was leaving Greensboro on my way home to Raleigh, a two hour trip, at the end of a long but good day, and I decided that it might be enjoyable to listen to some pleasant music as I drove along. I turned on the radio and began turning the dial. I couldn't find the kind of music I wanted, so I kept turning. At one point, I came upon what sounded like a hillbilly comedian telling jokes. I wasn't in the mood for that, so I went on to the end of the dial. Working my way back, I came to the comedian again. He evidently had just given a punchline because the audience was roaring. I decided to listen for a couple of minutes.

The comedian resumed, and he didn't go on for a minute before he mentioned the name of Jesus Christ. This surprised me. He obviously was not your run-of-the-mill comedian. His voice went soft and warm, and he went on for two or three minutes about what God could mean to people who truly loved Him. I got the feeling that he was talking to me and me alone. Then he threw in a self-deprecating one-liner that broke up the audience, and I had to laugh out loud. myself. I clicked on the casette recorder. Our company had grown to the size where we were having annual sales conventions attended by a couple hundred people, finishing with a banquet and a guest speaker. I didn't know who this comedian was, but I wanted to find out so we could invite him. I must have taped a half-hour of him before he finished. The audience gave him an ovation.

Over the applause, I heard the announcer say: "Ladies and gentlemen, you have just heard Dr. Norman Vincent Peale speaking to—"

Dr. Norman Vincent Peale!

I had never heard Dr. Peale speak before. If I had known who the speaker was, I would have expected him to be inspirational, which he was, but I didn't know he could be so humorous at the same time. I turned off the radio, re-wound the tape and played it again. I didn't realize I had laughed so much until I heard my own frequent laughter on the tape. When I got home, I played it for Carolyn, and she loved it, too. Next morning, I played it for some of my associates at the office.

When we had stopped laughing, I said: "Wouldn't it be terrific if we could get to Dr. Peale for our convention?"

Jerry Daly said: "Why don't you ask him?"

I shook my head. "No. We're too small. That crowd last

night must have had two or three thousand people in it. Dr. Peale wouldn't come down here for a convention our size."

That instant, the thought struck me to write Dr. Peale, letting him know how much I enjoyed his talk and how much I had gained from his books, not saying anything about the convention at all. I admired the man so much that if he answered my letter I knew I would have a souvenir I would treasure for life. The next instant, however, I decided not to write him. I knew he was a very busy man and probably received thousands of letters everyday. What was one more? Then the inner battle began in me—the gut feeling of nudging guidance, telling me to go ahead and write Dr. Peale, and the halting realism of conceding that he probably wouldn't answer, and the combat went on all day. As the time was nearing to go home, I just picked up a pencil and wrote the letter. I told Dr. Peale about hearing his broadcast, I told him how much I had benefited from his books, I told him some of the things the Lord was doing for our company and for me personally; I said that if he ever came south again I would like to meet him and that if I ever went north I hoped he'd give me an appointment. I didn't mention the convention. I gave the letter to my secretary and said: "Please type this up and let's get it in the mail right away before I change my mind again."

I was able to control my anticipation the first week—the fastest, I knew, that I could ordinarily expect a reply. The second week I was getting a little nervous. The third week I could hardly think of anything else. The fourth week I started getting a little disappointed. As the second month unfolded, I continued to go through my morning mail with a certain anxiety. Nothing. It was around the end of the second month that when I entered the office in the morning my secretary waved a piece of paper at me.

"It's from Dr. Peale," she said.

I hurried to her and grabbed it. The first thing I wanted to see was whether it was a form letter. It wasn't. The next thing I wanted to see was whether Dr. Peale himself had signed it. He had. Then when I read the letter I could see that it was personally from him. Among other things, he said that he had a heavy speaking schedule in the Midwest over the next few months and didn't know when we could meet but that he would have Ollie Porter, his assistant director of the Foundation for Christian Living, stop by and extend his personal regards. I wrote back that this would be fine with me. I was out of the office when Ollie Porter called a week or so later, so he spoke to J. L. Brooks and a lunch date was set up for the three of us. It was exciting to visit with somebody who knew Dr. Peale personally and worked for him. After we talked about Dr. Peale for a while, Ollie told us about the Foundation for Christian Living and what it was doing for the Lord in terms of publications, prayer groups and counseling. Then J.L. told Ollie about our own foundation.

At one point, Ollie Porter asked: "How do you support your foundation?"

I said: "Out of my personal earnings. How does Dr. Peale support his?"

"The foundation has become so big," he said, "that we have to depend mostly on donations."

"From where?"

"Individuals. Businesses, Other organizations."

"We give to organizations," I said. "Maybe we can help you."

"I was going to bring that up," Ollie said. "George, why don't you go up to Pawling, New York, and look the foundation over before you decide what you want to do?"

"Will I meet Dr. Peale?"

He thought about it. "The foundation always gets a lot of visitors, and when Dr. Peale is there he usually comes out of his office and shakes hands with everybody and visits for a few minutes."

I said: "I don't want to just shake hands with him. I want to have a talk with him."

He shrugged. "I can't promise anything, but I'll do my best."

"I'll settle for that."

When J.L. and I got back to the office, I talked to Jenk and said: "Jenk, I don't want to go all the way to Pawling to shake hands with Dr. Peale out in the hall. I'll wait and meet him some other time. You go up there and check out the foundation; and if you feel we ought to give them some money, let's do it."

Jenk made the trip and he came back on fire. He said: "It's a terrific organization. I had no idea it would be so large. They are helping thousands of people every day. I was amazed."

I asked: "Did you meet Dr. Peale?"

"Yes."

"Did you get a chance to talk to him?"

"I had him to myself in his office for two hours."

"What did you talk about for two hours?"

"I talked mostly about you. George, he wants to meet you."

"Did he say that?"

"Yes. I didn't have your appointments book with me, so I didn't know your schedule. But Dr. Peale wants me to call his office today and synchronize your two schedules and set up the meeting."

"You do that, Jenk," I said. "I want to meet this man very much."

"You will. And you'll love him," Jenk said. And then: "George, I want you to do something. When you go to Pawling, I want you to take along a check for ten thousand dollars. After you've looked over the foundation and after your meeting with Dr. Peale, if you're as excited as I am about the need they're filling and the man, contribute the check to the Foundation for Christian Living. They'll put it to good use, believe me."

"I'll do that," I said.

I was impressed by the foundation. I was overwhelmed by Norman Vincent Peale. I had him to myself in his office for two hours, too. We talked about everything, serious one moment, joking the next. We prayed together. When I began to wonder if I might be overstaying my welcome, I made a move to go, but Dr. Peale said: "Can you want a minute, George? I'd like to have a picture of us taken." He summoned a photographer and the picture was taken. I had my copy enlarged and framed, and I put it in my office. And when I gave them the check their gratitude was overwhelming.

As I was leaving, I said: "Dr. Peale, I'd like to feel that you and I are friends now."

"We are," he said.

I said: "I am still a country boy and once in a while I find myself in deep water. Can I come to you for advice whenever I need it?"

"Why wait for that?" he said. "Come and see me whenever you're in the neighborhood. I intend to go and see you whenever I'm in your neighborhood. We're both a couple of country boys."

I began to visit with Dr. Peale about once a month. I was fascinated by his foundation, so I asked if I could attend a couple of board meetings in order to pick up a few ideas for improving our own foundation. Next thing I knew, I was elected to the board myself.

One day Dr. Peale said to me: "George, next time you come to New York, let me know a few days in advance. I want you to have lunch with a friend of mine. I'm sure the two of you will like each other."

"All right," I said. "Who is he?"

"Lowell Thomas."

"Lowell Thomas the newscaster?"

"He's more than that, but that's the man."

"I've been a fan of his all my life."

"He's a fine man and a delightful person. I've told him about you and he said he'd like to meet you. You two should hit it off fine. He's a country boy, too."

A few weeks later, I had lunch with Lowell Thomas, and I sat there transfixed by this remarkable man throughout the entire meal. He kept trying to get me to talk about myself and I kept trying to get him to talk about himself. This is a wonderful way to start a friendship. The lunch was one of the high points of my life. I didn't know it at the time, but it was also the beginning of the consideration of me as a recipient of the Horatio Alger Award, since Dr. Peale was the president of the Horatio Alger Awards Committee and Lowell Thomas was an influential member of the board of directors.

A lingering low point of my life was the day the personnel director at the insurance company in Kannapolis told me I had no abilities to become a salesman, especially an insurance salesman. I didn't let it bug me, but whenever I'd remember the experience I'd growl, hoping that someday I could show this guy he was wrong.

I began thinking more and more about the insurance business. I knew it was a good business: every person in sight was a prospective customer. But the more I became attuned to the idea of going into the insurance business, the more I realized that I didn't know anything about it. At first, I thought of just opening my own insurance agency, but that would have meant starting from scratch and it could have been a long time before I'd build up a sizable company. Then I thought of going to one of the big companies and acquiring the representation for North Carolina. But that would have meant that I wouldn't be my own man, I'd have to go along with company policies, and I probably would not be allowed to resort to my own innovations to build up the business. Finally, I decided that the best thing to do would be to buy a small company on the way up and start the long haul of building. I nosed around and learned there were three or four companies that would consider selling out. But this was new territory for me, and I didn't want to stumble ahead on my own and make a lot of mistakes. I thought about it and asked the opinion of my associates and other professionals.

I was with Norman Vincent Peale one day and brought up the subject, and he said: "Well, then, what you need is some advice from somebody who is already successful in insurance." He called his secretary and said: "See if you can get me Clem Stone in Chicago, please." W. Clement Stone was a hero of mine. His books had helped me a lot. He had become a multimillionaire in the insurance business, but that wasn't what I admired about him most. I liked his motivation, I liked his positive attitudes, I liked his pride in being a salesman, despite the fact that he had built an insurance empire, and I liked his acknowledgment of the Lord in his life.

The secretary came back in a few minutes and said: "Mr. Stone is on a trip and won't be back in Chicago for several weeks."

Dr. Peale looked at me. "Can this wait?"

I said: "Well, Dr. Peale, when I become interested in something, I like to get moving on it right away."

"Me, too," he said. "Okay. I'll contact some people I know in the insurance business and be back in touch with you. You can take it from there."

He wrote to Jim Bingay, president of Mutual of New York; Henry Smith, president and chief executive officer of Equitable Assurance of New York; and Charlie Zimmerman, chief executive officer of Connecticut Mutual. Without Norman Vincent Peale, I wouldn't have had a chance in the world of getting near the door of the offices of these men, but thanks to him they received me, gave me all the time I wanted, plus a lot of very important advice. Jim Bingay suggested that I work with a stock company which would enhance our opportunities. It was also recommended that I get in touch with somebody with experience in insurance companies at the level where I wanted to start, someone who could size up the situation and advise us about which way to go. I did. He was a man with twenty years of experience in running agencies all over the country. He knew the insurance business inside and out.

He came down to Raleigh and spent a few days. He studied all the data we had, asked us a lot of questions and made a lot of phone calls. He then advised us to go ahead into the insurance on the basis of our plans and he gave us a profile of the sort of man we should find to run the insurance department of our company.

So we launched the insurance division of our organization.

At the presentation of the Horatio Alger Awards on October 17, 1975, it was Dr. Peale who introduced each recipient and said a few words about him or her. When it was my turn, I went and stood beside him at the podium as he identified me, and then he said: "At seventy-four, George Shinn is the youngest person to receive the Horatio Alger Award." There was some laughter from the audience. Dr. Peale looked around to see what had happened.

I whispered to him: "Thirty-four. I'm thirty-four."

In his regular voice, he asked: "What did I say?"

"You said seventy-four."

"Oh," he said, looking at the audience. "I must have been thinking about myself. But I don't have his millions."

Millions don't mean much when your reputation is being threatened. Somewhere I've read: "He who loses his wealth loses little. He who loses his health loses much. He who loses his reputation loses everything." That almost happened to me.

As a result of the Horatio Alger Award, I got a lot of publicity, and I started getting many more invitations to speak to business groups, youth groups, and churches. I enjoyed doing this because it gave me an opportunity to acknowledge publicly what God had done for me, plus the hope that maybe I could persuade other people to seek the Lord. In December, 1975, about two months after the awards, I was in Arkansas. It was a Friday, I remember. I was scheduled to speak that morning at the Southern Baptist College. At noon, I was to speak to the Kiwanis Club, and that evening I was to be the main speaker at the Southern Senators Annual Banquet. The talk at the college had gone well. Around eleven-thirty in the morning, I received a call from my office, and I got the shock of my life. This is what happened.

Four years before, an employee of one of our schools had allegedly falsified some records, in that he reportedly registered as a student at the school a friend of his who was eligible for G.I. Bill assistance through the Veterans Administration. Working in the office was a woman who knew what had gone on. She informed the V.A., and the V.A. turned the matter over to the Attorney General. The F.B.I. went to work to check out the situation, and that was how newspaper reporters learned about the incident.

The story hit the front pages. The main thrust of the stories was not that a crime had possibly been committed by a college employee, but that the college was owned by George Shinn, self-made millionaire at thirty-four, recent recipient of the Horatio Alger Award. Overnight, I went (in many people's minds) from the fair-haired boy of North Carolina to the state's Public Enemy Number One. Most of the accounts didn't even mention the name of the employee involved. It was all George Shinn, as though I was the one being investigated by the F.B.I.

I don't know how I got through the luncheon speech with the Kiwanis Club. I spent all afternoon on the phone, contacting the members of our company's executive board who were traveling all over the country and asking them to meet me at headquarters in the morning. Somehow I got through the evening with the southern senators. I flew back to Raleigh that night.

At the board meeting Saturday morning, I decided to tell the members what was in my heart. I had known the person involved for ten years, I considered him a good friend, and I sincerely loved him. About a year after he supposedly made the falsification, he had turned his life over to the Lord, and I was sure that if he had been faced with the temptation since then he would have resisted it. If it had been my own money that had been misappropriated, I would have dismissed the entire incident, especially now since the man had a change of heart. But Uncle Sam's money was involved, however little of it, and Uncle Sam had the right of retribution and the application of the law. If it turned out that the man had to go to jail for what happened, I would certainly see to it that his family didn't go hungry. But the man and his family were not the only people involved. For reasons I still don't understand, the newspaper reporters had involved me, our company and all of our people in all of our areas of activity, and incredibly, Norman Vincent Peale and the Horatio Alger Awards. A lot of people were being hurt. In view of this, I could see no other course of action but to dissassociate the man from the company. The board agreed.

I phoned the man at his home and asked him to meet me in a couple of hours, the time it would take me to drive there from Raleigh. I had tears in my eyes as I fired him. We prayed together and I told him to have faith and to remember that all things work together for good to those that love the Lord.

I was scheduled to speak the next morning at the Centerview Baptist Church in Kannapolis, my mother's church, and so I drove on to Kannapolis, arriving just in time for dinner. By this time, I was able to fulfill the promise I had made the preacher after my father's funeral, to take care of my mother. She had stopped working five years before. She had a nice home and a new car now.

When I entered my mother's house, she said: "A woman by the name of Mrs. Ware has been calling you all day."

I said: "Who is she?"

Mother said: "I don't know. She left her number and she wants you to call her."

"I'm not in the mood to talk to strangers," I said, but I didn't say why.

We had dinner and then went to spend the evening with Carolyn's parents, returning to Mother's place around ten. Almost immediately, the phone rang. Mother said: "That's probably Mrs. Ware again."

"If it is," I said, "tell her that I'm not here."

Mother said: "Junior, I'm not going to lie for you or anybody else. If it's Mrs. Ware, I'll tell her you're here and you can tell her yourself that you don't want to talk to her."

It was Mrs. Ware. I took the phone and asked: "What can I do for you, Mrs. Ware?"

"It's what I can do for you," she said, going on: "George, we don't know each other, but all day today the Lord has been pushing me to get in touch with you."

"What about, Mrs. Ware?"

"Well," she said, "I've been reading about you in the papers, about the wonderful award you got and about all the good you are doing for people. I'm sure you must be a fine Christian man, and I've been praying for you."

I said: "Thank you, Mrs. Ware. Is that what you wanted to tell me?"

"No," she said. "It's this. When a man of God starts getting rich and famous the devil starts doing all he can to cause him trouble. I know you don't have any problems right now, George, but they're going to start coming."

The Kannapolis paper had not picked up the story about the problems in the nearby city. I said: "I'll watch my step, Mrs. Ware."

"That's not the point," she said. "Don't lose your faith in God. Keep your faith. A lot of people fall away from God when they start having problems, and then He can't reach them to help them. Keep your faith, George."

It was like being shot between the eyes. That moment, I realized that I hadn't prayed all day, not even my morning greeting to the Lord. I said: "Mrs. Ware, you'll never know how much I appreciate this call. As it happens, some problems have come up in the past couple of days, something that could be very embarrassing to me and my company. So I appreciate your message, and I'm sure going to need your prayers."

"And say your own prayers," she said. "God put you on top of the mountain. Now you are down in the valley. But do you know who can put you back on top of the mountain?"

"God can."

"Yes, as long as you trust Him and love Him and serve Him."

We talked for over an hour. At one point, Mrs. Ware simply announced that she was going to say a prayer for me, and she went into a beautiful prayer that was right on the button, touching my heart and restoring my spirits.

Finally, I said: "Mrs. Ware, I want to meet you. I'm speaking in the morning at the Centerview Baptist Church and I'm going to tell the people about this call. I'd like for you to be there. Can you make it?"

"Well, I'd like to, George," she said, "but it would be a little difficult for me to get over there."

"I'll send somebody over to pick you up," I said.

"Well, that's not the problem," she said. "I'm in a wheelchair, George. And it would be much better to hear you the next time you speak in the area."

And I thought I had problems. I said: "I have to head back to Raleigh right after the service tomorrow, but the next time I'm in Kannapolis I'll get in touch with you."

"I'll be in touch with you before then. I'll be in touch with you everyday," she said, "with my prayers."

I needed a lot of prayers.

The reporters wouldn't let up. I called a press conference, which turned out to be a mistake. I tried to establish that I was not involved in the misappropriation in any way whatsoever, that it had taken place four years before and I found out about it four days before, and that the F.B.I. was examining the school's records but not me personally. And I tried to do this without saying anything that would be harmful to the former employee in any legal action facing him. The result was a batch of articles that were vague, confused, contradictory and always accusative.

A reporter came to interview me in my office. When he saw the picture of Dr. Peale and me that was taken the day we met, he said: "I understand that Dr. Peale is the head of the Horatio Alger Awards."

I said: "That's right."

He said: "I also understand that you have given Dr. Peale a lot of money."

I said: "That's inaccurate. My foundation gave Dr. Peale's foundation some money so that he could carry on his Christian work. If you want to look at our books, you'll see that we have given money to many organizations for the same reason."

He brushed the offer aside, asking: "Is there any connection between the donation and the award?"

I wanted to hit him. I said: "If I thought there was, I wouldn't have accepted the award; and if I find out there was, I'll give the award back."

The article that came out bore little resemblance to the actual conversation.

I didn't know whether anybody was trying to reach Dr. Peale for a statement, so I went up to New York and told him everything that was going on. He listened to me attentively and sympathetically, assuring me that he wouldn't make a statement on it to anybody, and then he said: "I've been through something like that myself, George, so I know what an ordeal it can be."

It appears that when Dr. Peale's book on positive thinking came out, he was attacked by the clergy of all denominations, condemning him for trying to relate personal success to Christian living. "They were brutal," he told me. "Every day for months, some publication would carry some assault on me, and then a reporter would come around and ask if I wanted to make a rebuttal. I didn't, hoping that if I kept quiet the whole thing would wither and go away. But it went on and on.

"And it kept getting worse," he said. "Not only did the critics blast me and the book, but they also blasted the publisher, they blasted Marble Collegiate Church where I am the pastor, and they blasted *Guidepost Magazine*, which I edit. And I kept sinking lower and lower into depression. Things got so bad that I seriously considered resigning from the church. I talked to my wife about it, but Ruth refused to advise me in any direction.

"But I knew I needed advice, and I felt the only other person besides Ruth whose advise I could trust was my father. He was a retired minister himself then, living in Ohio, so I went out there and told him the whole story, telling him what I was thinking of doing depending on how he felt about it.

"He thought about it for a few moments, then asked: 'Have you told me everything?'

"I said: 'Yes, I have.'

"He said: 'You're not holding back on anything to spare me?'

"I said: 'No, Dad.'

"He said: 'Do you feel that in your work you are doing what's right and good?'

"I said: 'Yes.'

"He asked: 'Are you teaching the Gospel of our Lord Jesus Christ?'

"I said: 'Yes, I am.'

"He said: 'Then as long as you are teaching the Gospel of our Lord Jesus Christ, you go right on with your work, and you can just tell all those other people that they can jump in the lake.' "

When Dr. Peale got to the punchline, he laughed harder than I had ever seen him laugh before, and this is a man who laughs easily. I had to laugh myself, maybe at myself.

When I thought about that advice, I remembered some similar advice I had once been given. It was at the time my business was on the verge of bankruptcy. I happened to be in Concord one day, and I went to see a man, an older and wiser man, whom I had come to know while I was working at the school there. I told him about my problems and said I didn't know what to do about them. He said: "George, you're not giving God enough time."

"What do you mean?" I asked.

"Look at it this way," he said. "Have you ever gone for a

walk in the woods and come upon a creek in which the water looked so fresh and clean and pure that you could scoop it up with your hands and drink it?"

"Yes," I said. "That happened to me many times when I was a kid."

He said: "Well, let's say that it happened to you today. And let's say that you go back there and you see that some farmer had driven his cows across the creek and one cow dropped some manure. Would you drink the water then?"

"Of course not."

"Okay. So let's say you go back to the creek in another week and you see that the swift current of the creek had swept all the dirt away and the water was once again fresh and clean and pure. Would you drink some then?"

"Probably."

"Of course you would," he said. "Well, George, the powers of God are like the swift current of that creek. No matter what problems drop into your life, just give God enough time and He will sweep them away. Just give Him the time."

So I decided to combine those two pieces of advice— letting the reporters go their merry way and giving God all the time He wanted.

About a year later, in September, 1976, indictments were handed down against the former employee. The school itself and I personally were completely exonerated. Even so, I was a bit apprehensive when I picked up the newspapers that day. But all was well. The reports were accurate. The storm was over. Maybe the experience wouldn't have been so stormy for me if I had learned earlier to give the Lord His time.

The more time I gave God, the more time I spent thinking about Him, praying to Him, showing Him I loved Him, the more I realized that personal success has a distinct pattern, at least for me, and it is the pattern of a triangle. For me it has become the triangle to success: the one side of the triangle symbolizes attitudes—positive, creative, aggressive attitudes in everything you do. If you start out on a project feeling that you will never complete it or that it will fail, that's what can happen to you. But if you start out convinced that you are a winner, that can happen to you, too. The second side of the triangle symbolizes good health. My bad back and my other problems taught me the importance of good health—regular check-ups, daily exercise and proper diet. If you don't have good health, you won't have the energy and strength to carry out your attitudes, whatever they are. But the most important part of the triangle is the third side, the base, the foundation, which is Jesus Christ. If your whole life isn't based on Jesus Christ, you can think you are a winner and you can be in the best of health, but you will just keep running around in circles. Jesus Christ gives you direction, purpose and lasting achievements.

For me, personal success is not a matter of wealth and fame. Personal success is simply the fulfillment of what makes you happiest. A fulfilled housewife is a success. A fulfilled truckdriver is a success. A fulfilled athlete is a success. A fulfilled business executive is a success. A shared love is a success.

It would be unrealistic to suggest that the successful person is always living at the top of the mountain. We all have our valleys. We all experience tragedies. We all have setbacks. We all make mistakes in judgments of people and situations—the Lord knows I've made mine. But these valleys can be learning experiences, learning more about others, about ourselves, about the Lord. Without Him, there can be no mountains.

A lot of people wince when I emphasize the importance of God in personal success. They tell me that they have never been of a religious bent and they don't have the inclination to become a theologian. God doesn't expect us all to become theologians. God just wants us to acknowledge Him, to love Him and serve Him, to treat others the way we would want them to treat us, and to turn to Him in good times as well as in bad times. That doesn't take a lot of work. In fact, getting started is easy.

When you wake up tomorrow morning, go to the window, smile at the wonderful world no matter what kind of a day it is, and proclaim:

"Good morning, Lord!"